State Formation in Early China

DUCKWORTH DEBATES IN ARCHAEOLOGY

Series editor: Richard Hodges

Also available

State Formation
in
Early China

Li Liu & Xingcan Chen

Duckworth

First published in 2003 by
Gerald Duckworth & Co. Ltd.
90-93 Cowcross Street, London EC1M 6BF
Tel: 020 7490 7300
Fax: 020 7490 0080
inquiries@duckworth-publishers.co.uk
www.ducknet.co.uk

A catalogue record for this book is available
from the British Library

ISBN 0 7156 3224 8

Typeset by Ray Davies
Printed in Great Britain by
Biddles Ltd, *www.biddles.co.uk*

Contents

Dedicated to Professor Kwang-chih Chang

Acknowledgements

Much of the data used in this book is based on the results from two projects. One is an investigation of copper and salt resources in the Zhongtiao Mountains region in southern Shanxi, conducted by the authors in 1999; and the other is the Yiluo region survey project carried out since 1998 by an international collaborative research team, including the authors. The Cultural Heritage Preservation and the Archaeology Department of the National Cultural Relics Bureau of China, the Institute of Archaeology of the Chinese Academy of Social Sciences, and the Henan Provincial Cultural Relics Bureau have been extremely supportive of our research. Our deepest appreciation goes to archaeologists and historians, Zhang Yanhuang, Song Xinchao, Guan Qiang, Shi Jinming, Li Baiqin, Zheng Guang, Xu Hong, Chen Liangwei, Du Jinpeng, Wang Xuerong, Tang Jigen, Ma Xiaolin, Liao Yongmin, Liu Hongmiao, Fang Hui, and Chai Jiguang, who provided generous assistance and information. We are grateful to our Yiluo project team members, Yun Kuen Lee, Henry Wright, Arlene Rosen, Huang Weidong, Li Yongqiang, Wang Hongzhang, and Wang Facheng, from whom we benefit in interdisciplinary approaches. David Keightley and Lothar von Falkenhausen reviewed the manuscript and provided invaluable and constructive comments. We especially thank Wei Ming for his high-quality illustrations and Susan Bridekirk who edited the manuscript. La Trobe University funded the copper-salt project; and the Australian Research Council, the National Geographic Foundation, and the Wenner-Gren Foundation have supported the Yiluo survey project. Without support and help from the above individuals and institutions the completion of this research would have been impossible. However, we are responsible for all imperfections in this work.

List of Figures

List of Figures

	City-states (Yates and Lin)	Segmentary states (Southall and Keightley)	Territorial states and village states (Trigger and Maisels)	Archaeological evidence discussed in this study
Political organization	Shang territory small; many 'fang' regional polities coexist with Shang	Shang ritual suzerainty extends widely but political sovereignty limited	Shang kings journey across a large region; move capitals to control a large territory; resettle farming populations to remote regions	Politically centralized polities with large territories; political expansion from core to periphery in order to control key resources such as metal and salt
Urban structure	Shang cities as cult centres, but no evidence indicates farmers were not in Shang cities	Shang cities as cult centres	Relatively small population including the ruling Shang capitals as centres of cult and elite craft production	Major centres at Erlitou and Zhengzhou as religious, political, and economic centres; population at major centres including elites, craftsmen, and peasants
Defensibility in capital	Although Shang ritual centres were not walled, many other sites were		Unwalled capitals located in centre of large unified territory	Erlitou not fortified, but Yanshi, Zhengzhou and Huanbei were fortified
Economic structure	Shang bureaucracy was minimal; unclear if peasants paid taxes, rents, and corvée labour duties to urban elite	Shang bureaucracy was minimal; unclear if peasants paid taxes, rents, and corvée labour duties to urban elite	Tributary; two-tiered economy: frequently resettle farming population due to intensive agricultural production in Shang	Tributary economy rather than market and trade; tributary items from periphery including both prestige and utilitarian goods

Table 1. Applications of general models of early states to the Shang, compared with archaeological data discussed in this study

Table 2. Chronology of major archaeological sites mentioned in the text

Dynasty	Dates BC*	Archaeological phase	Eritou	Yanshi	Zhengzhou	Anyang	Yuanqu	Dongxia-feng	Dongjiong-shan	Laonupo	Panlongcheng	Wucheng	Daxinzhuang	Zhukaigou	Shimen
Late Shang	1046 - 1220	Yinxu				× ◆ ▽				× ◆		□ ◆	×		
Middle Shang		Transitional Period (Huanbei)				× □ ▽ Huanbei				× ◆	× □ ◆	× ◆	×		
	1435	Late Upper Erligang (Baijiazhuang)	×	× □	× ◆ ▽ (?) Xiaoshuang-qiao			× □	×	× ◆	× □ ◆	× ◆	×	× ◆	× ◆
Early Shang		Early Upper Erligang	×	× □	× □ ◆ ▽		× □ ◆	× □	×	× ◆	× □ ◆	× ◆	×	× ◆	× ◆
		Late Lower Erligang	×	× □	× □ ◆ ▽		× □ ◆	× □ ◆	×	× ◆	× ◆				
		Early Lower Erligang	×	× □	× □ ◆ ▽		× ◆	× □ ◆	×	× ◆	× ◆				
	1600	Erlitou IV	⊗ ◆ ▽	⊗ × □ ◆			⊗ ◆	⊗ ◆	⊗		⊗				
		Erlitou III	⊗ ◆ ▽				⊗ ◆	⊗ ◆	⊗		⊗				
Xia		Erlitou II	⊗ ◆ ▽					⊗							
	1900	Erlitou I	⊗												

⊗ Presence of the Erlitou culture
× Presence of the Erligang and Shang culture
□ Presence of walled enclosure
◆ Presence of bronze metallurgy (mining, smelting, or casting)
▽ Location of primary centre
* Dates based on the results of AMS and regular C-14 dating reported in the Three Dynasties Chronology Project (Xia Shang Zhou 2000).

11

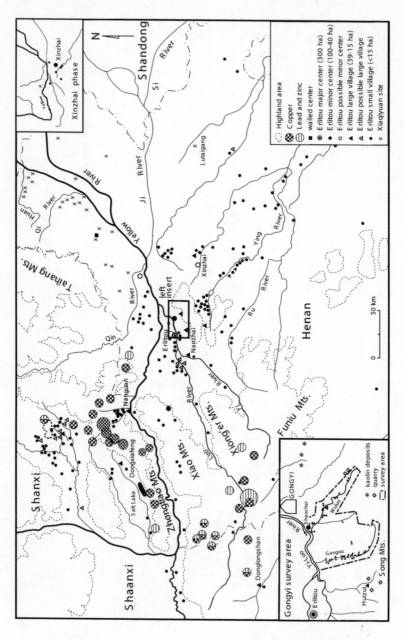

Figure 1. Distribution of the Erlitou and Xiaqiyuan sites, geographical setting, and locations of key natural resources

Introduction

China is one of the most ancient civilizations in the world, but there is little consensus among scholars concerning specific issues – such as dates, locations, identities of participants – involved in the developmental processes of the earliest urbanism and state-level society in this part of the world. Many Western anthropologists, archaeologists, and historians have attempted to characterize early states in China by reference to broad theoretical categories of social formation derived from a comparative perspective on world history. On the other hand, many Chinese scholars have been obsessed with historically orientated research, primarily for reconstructing Chinese national history. It is not surprising, therefore, that the two groups have experienced difficulties in finding each other's arguments particularly helpful. Language barriers have created further obstacles, causing, for the Chinese, lack of participation in discussions on a general theoretical level, and for Western theorists, lack of access to recent archaeological information.

Kwang-chih Chang was one of the pioneers who made great efforts to bridge the gap between general Western social theories and the rapidly growing wealth of archaeological information coming out of China. During the 1960s and 1970s he stood at the forefront of American anthropology in regard to archaeological theory, and was a leader both in general methodological debates in archaeology and in the study of settlement patterns. By actively participating in the mainstream of American

13

anthropological archaeology, he was able to interpret Chinese archaeological data from a new perspective.

Chang paid particular attention to the nature and dynamics of the early states in China, especially in the Shang dynasty (*c.* 1600-1046 BC). His discussion of the transitional processes of Chinese civilization, which differed from those of Mesopotamian civilization (Chang 1984), was based largely on his systematic research into the social formation of the Shang dynasty (Chang 1980) and many related issues concerning the development of urbanism (Chang 1976, 1985) and the acquisition of power (Chang 1983). He argued that there was a connection between the demand for raw material resources and the locations of Shang cities, and, in particular, that the capital cities of early states in northern China may have played important roles in the procurement and protection of copper and tin mines and in the transportation of copper/tin ingots (Chang 1976, 1985). Location changes of the capital cities of the Three Dynasties, therefore, were presumably caused by the frequent exhaustion of the copper and tin mines in north China and the consequent incessant pursuit of new sources of these metals (Chang 1986: 367). He also suggested that the strategic importance of southern Shanxi to the early states was the result of its possession of the largest salt resources in the region (Chang 1980: 258).

All these arguments, which brought fresh air as well as new debate into Chinese archaeology, have inspired our research on state formation in early China, the topic of this book. Since there is far more archaeological data available today than Professor Chang had when he discussed these topics nearly twenty years ago, some of our conclusions are different from his. However, the results of our research, as presented in this book, are but the extension and elaboration of issues initially explored by Kwang-chih Chang.

1

Early States: Theoretical
Models and Applications

Early states in different parts of the world vary in configuration
and have been characterized by some anthropologists in several
major forms. The most recurrent forms are city-states (Nichols
and Charlton 1997; Trigger 1993), segmentary states (Southall
1956, 1988), territorial states (Trigger 1993), and village-states
(Maisels 1987, 1990). Scholars have attempted to apply these
generalizations to interpretations of early Chinese civilization
from a cross-cultural comparative perspective (Keightley 2000;
Lin 1998; Maisels 1987, 1990; Southall 1993; Trigger 1999;
Yates 1997). These models, focusing mainly on the Shang and
Western Zhou dynasties, may be briefly summarized as follows.

The city-states model

City-states are the earliest and most recurrent form of state in
the primary civilizations of the Near East, Asia, Europe and the
Americas, with dates ranging from 4000 BC to AD 1600
(Charlton and Nichols 1997). As defined by Trigger, city-states
were governed by hereditary kingship and territories were
small, covering a few hundred square kilometres. They had a
three-tier settlement hierarchy, including the capital, small
centres, and villages. Capital cities were frequently walled for
defensive purposes, and the great majority of the population,
including farmers, resided in capital cities (up to 80% in the case

15

of Sumer). Craft production and technology were highly developed, and substantial market activity took place within city-states. Farming was intensive, but surpluses were low. Adjacent city-states often competed militarily for control of farmland along their borders, and for control of trade routes and other resources (Trigger 1993).

Yates (1997) notes that the concept of the city-state is particularly useful in the case of ancient China, as it corresponds more closely to the way in which the ancient Chinese understood their settlements than any other model. In ancient illustrations, several terms describe elements of settlement organization, including *yi* (walled settlements), *guo* (area within the city wall), and *ye* (the borders of the kingdom), and taken altogether constitute a domain, similar to a city-state (ibid.: 83). Scholars have observed some characteristics of the Shang dynasty which indicate that it may have been similar to the city-states model, including the following. It is not clear how much actual territory the Shang controlled at any one point in time; in fact Keightley (1983: 548) has argued that the Shang dynasty may have been a network of pathways and encampments rather than a large unified political entity. Bureaucracy in the Shang dynasty may have been minimal (ibid.: 557-8), so it cannot be asserted that the main economic link between urban and rural sectors was maintained through peasants paying taxes, rents, and corvée labour duties to the urban elite. In this way the Shang dynasty was not like a territorial state. There is no archaeological evidence to indicate that farmers did not live next to artisans and craftsmen in walled sites. And lastly, while some centres of ritual activity do not appear to be walled, many sites were (Yates 1997).

Yates emphasized that kinship ties were the basis of the social structure of these early states, and that ancestor worship was one of the most potent legitimizing forces for the regime. These phenomena, he argues, seem close to the model that

16

Tambiah (1977, 1985) described as 'galactic polity' for Southeast Asia, in which law was not significant for the creation of the state, but ritual played an essential role in the political process and the formation of settlement hierarchy. According to Yates, the application of the concept of city-states to ancient China should therefore be integrated into the model of the galactic polity.

Lin Yun has also employed the city-states model to describe political organization during the Shang dynasty. After examining the concept of *fang* (see below) in oracle-bone inscriptions, Lin suggested that these *fang*s may have been independent polities on the periphery, whose relationships with the Shang varied from hostile to allied, and that it may have been the state confederation which characterized the relationship between the Shang dynasty and those allied *fang* polities (Lin 1998).

The segmentary states model

Segmentary states, according to Southall, are those in which 'territorial sovereignty is recognized but limited and essentially relative, forming a series of zones in which authority is most absolute near the centre and increasingly restricted towards the periphery, often shading off into a ritual hegemony' (Southall 1956: 248). Ritual suzerainty extends widely towards a flexible, changing periphery, while political sovereignty is confined to the central, core domain (Southall 1988: 52). This model, extensively discussed in the study of African and South Asian states (Southall 1956, 1988, 1991, 1999; Stein 1977, 1980), has been used to interpret the Shang political landscape (Keightley 2000; Southall 1993: 33).

Keightley argues that in the Shang people's minds there were three concepts relating to their political geography as demonstrated in oracle-bone inscriptions. There was *Da yi Shang*, 'the great settlement Shang', which may have referred to the combined cult centre and capital at Xiaotun; this centre,

17

however, had not yet assumed the central political and bureau-cratic role that it had in later Chinese capitals. There was *situ*, 'the Four Lands', which were the Shang domain immediately surrounding the cult centre. There was *fang*, 'border, country, or region', which was used to refer to non-Shang or enemy groups outside the Shang domain (Keightley 2000: 56-72). According to Keightley (1979-80: 26): 'it is unlikely that the full Shang state, except at its centre, can be associated with a defined and bounded territory ... The state itself was conceived of, not as Shang territory, but as a series of pro-Shang jurisdictions, each with its particular relationship to the centre'. Local rulers were bound to the Shang only by varying and mutable ties of kinship, religious belief, or self-interest. Although the political geogra-phy of relationships between the Shang dynasty and these local rulers cannot yet be determined with precision, the various descent groups that were allied at one time or another with the dynasty were small, distributed mainly in northern and north-western Henan and in southeastern Shanxi along the Yellow and Qin rivers (Keightley 2000: 56-8). Over 500 Shang sites have been identified in a large region including Henan, Hebei, and Shanxi. Shaanxi, Anhui, Shandong, Jiangsu, Zhejiang, Hubei, Jiangxi, Hunan, Sichuan, Inner Mongolia, Liaoning, and other provinces. These archaeological sites that were culturally Shang, however, were not necessarily politically Shang (Keightley 1999: 275-7).

In many respects the segmentary state model is similar to the city-state model. Both Yates and Keightley agree that the political domain of the Shang dynasty was relatively small, and that bureaucracy in the capital was minimal.

The territorial-states model

Bruce Trigger has defined the concept of the territorial state as a political entity with a single ruler who controlled a large area through a hierarchy of provincial and local administrators and

administrative centres. Urban centres were small and inhabited almost exclusively by administrators, elite specialists, and
retainers, while farmers lived in dispersed homesteads and
villages. Territorial states tended to have a clearly separated
two-tier economy: while farmers manufactured what they
needed from locally-available raw materials on a part-time
basis and exchanged these goods among themselves, elite
craftsmen, living in cities or on royal estates, manufactured
luxury goods for the king and upper classes, often from exotic
materials. Urban centres obtained food almost exclusively as
rents or taxes from local communities (Trigger 1993: 10-11,
1999).

In his discussion of cross-cultural comparison, Trigger points
out that several characteristics of the Shang dynasty are similar to other large territorial states, from Egypt to Peru. First,
territorial states tend to have multiple capitals, the result of the
shifting location of capitals from one period to another. These
shifts resulted from the slowness of communications (limited by
technology), which made it difficult to govern a large area from
a single centre. The frequent relocation of capitals during the
early Shang dynasty and the simultaneous use of multiple
capitals in the late Shang dynasty, noted by Trigger, seems to
support this hypothesis. It is generally assumed that the relocation of capitals during the Shang dynasty was motivated by
military considerations related to the expansion or maintenance of unity within the realm. Secondly, royal travel
patterns of the late Shang dynasty, recorded on oracle-bone
inscriptions, indicate that kings journeyed across large regions
within a unified territorial state. Thirdly, in territorial states
capitals were not walled because there was little need for
defence against external attack in the centre of a large territory.
Public buildings and elite residences were, however, often surrounded by high walls to ensure privacy and security. These
characteristics of community pattern are observable in the

Shang capitals of Zhengzhou and Anyang. Fourthly, in territorial states agricultural production was not intensive, and rulers frequently resettled farming populations in an effort to develop remote and sparsely populated parts of their kingdoms. These phenomena can also be seen in the patterns of Shang dynasty settlement expansion. Finally, a large number of bronze ritual vessels, made primarily for the elites of the Shang dynasty, resemble the situation in other examples of territorial states, in which elite craft items were produced for the king and high state officials, rather than for the general market (Trigger 1999: 52-8).

The village-states model

Based on an earlier Marxist concept, the 'Asiatic' mode of production (Brook 1989; Godelier 1978; Marx 1973), Maisels proposed the 'village-state' as a general pattern found in early states in East Asia, in contrast to the city-states system particularly used to describe Mesopotamian settlements (Maisels 1987, 1990). The village-state is a royal, administrative, and cultic centre, surrounded by a sea of peasant villages that produced similar subsistence crops by similar methods over an extensive and largely uniform terrain (Maisels 1990: 255). In such societies subordinate social classes were formed at the base of the conical clans with the segmentary lineage intact, and thus without private property in the means of production (Maisels 1987: 354).

Maisels analyzed Shang and Zhou dynasty urban sites and argued that they were large, sprawling, and with few architectural remains, and that their societies were organized primarily on the conical kinship system. Chinese states, therefore, manifest a complete contrast in all these respects to the cities of ancient Mesopotamia, which were economic and population centres with a hereditary kingship system. Chinese states, according to Maisels, were essentially political and cultic, and not economic centres, as they drew revenues from a wide area populated by basically autarkic villages producing very similar items by largely identical methods. These characteristics, he argued, are shared with those defined as the village-state mode of production (Maisels 1990: 12-13, 254-61).

The concepts of the territorial state and village-state are similar. They both regard early states in China as large territories dominated by a centralized political entity.

Problems with the models and alternative approaches

These four models can be grouped into two camps, city-states and segmentary states on the one hand; territorial-states and village-states on the other. Major disputes between the two camps are concerned with the political structure and the size of the territory of the late Shang dynasty: whether or not the Shang controlled a territory large enough to qualify the dynasty as a centralized polity. Crucial to the resolution of this dispute is some understanding of the relationship between the distribution of a material culture and the administrative territory of a polity. Keightley (1983, 1999) pointed out that these two categories do not overlap in the case of the Shang dynasty, in that its influence in material culture (which is archaeologically visible) spatially exceeded its administrative boundaries (which are revealed in oracle-bone inscriptions) (Keightley 1983: map 17.3). Trigger and Maisels seem to be less concerned with this problem; they emphasize the general pattern of a royal administrative and cultic centre surrounded by subordinate settlements over extensive terrain (Maisels 1990: 255), with the assumption of some level of integration between the centre and periphery (Trigger 1990: 45).

The territorial/village models, which favour a large unified political entity for the Shang dynasty, are consistent with the views of many Chinese historians and archaeologists today (e.g. Li 1997b; Song 1991; Wang 1998). On the other hand, the city-/segmentary state models interpret early states in China as formations of a number of coexisting small polities. Many Western historians and archaeologists who study the political systems of the Shang dynasty share the view that Shang territory was smaller in size than traditionally believed, and that non-Shang political entities on the periphery were not as backward as has been recorded in ancient texts, that many polities contemporary with the Shang dynasty may have been autonomous states, and that among these the Shang dynasty was the strongest (e.g. Bagley 1999; Shaughnessy 1989; Shelach 1996). Table 1 on p. 10 above compares the theoretical camps and their applications to the Shang dynasty.

Furthermore, many archaeologists and historians, especially in China, believe that the Erlitou culture, which was centred in the Yiluo basin in western Henan and extended archaeologically to a much larger region, represents a later development of the first dynasty in China, the Xia (*c.* 2100-1600 BC) (e.g. Chang 1999: 71-3; Du 1991; Gao *et al.* 1998; Zhao 1987; Zou 1980). Many Chinese scholars accept that the Xia and Shang dynasties were state-level societies that constituted large centralized political systems throughout their reigns (e.g. Li 1997b; Song 1991; Wang 1998). These views are not shared by all Western archaeologists and historians, some of whom are sceptical about the historical connection between the Erlitou and the Xia, and question whether or not the Erlitou culture represented a state-level polity (e.g. Allan 1984; Bagley 1999: 130-1; Keightley 1983; Linduff 1998: 629; Railey 1999: 178-86; Thorp 1991).

These interpretations of the political organization in early Chinese civilization regarding the nature of the Erlitou culture and Shang state appear to be contradictory. The reasons for such a situation are complex. Different emphasis and selection of data in research (e.g. ideological or material, economic or religious) may affect the understanding of the ancient societies in question. Different sources of information (archaeological or textual) used by researchers can lead to different interpretations. Different cultural and educational backgrounds of scholars in China and the West may also contribute to their research orientations and biased views of Chinese history (e.g. Bagley 1999: 124-36; Falkenhausen 1995). In addition, most of the discussions by Western scholars are based on limited archaeological information published a few decades ago and on ancient texts including oracle-bone inscriptions. For instance, both Trigger and Maisels make their conclusions about early urban morphology based on Paul Wheatley's (1971) concept of the 'ceremonial complex', which characterized the earliest urban centres in the Shang dynasty. According to Wheatley, Zhengzhou and Anyang were political and ritual centres; each comprised a centrally situated ceremonial and administrative enclave occupied mainly by those of royal lineage, priests, and a few selected craftsmen. The villages which provided material subsistence, on the other hand, were dispersed through the surrounding countryside (Wheatley 1971: 47). Wheatley's widely accepted generalization was derived largely from textual information and archaeological evidence from before the 1970s. At that time Zhengzhou was thought to be surrounded by a rammed-earth enclosure which separated palatial areas from craft workshops and residential sites. But a recent discovery of a section of outer wall, demarcating a more extensive urban boundary, has altered our understanding of the Zhengzhou urban layout, suggesting that the outer walls also surrounded craft workshops and commoners' residences. Wheatley's concept of a ceremonial complex, therefore, needs to be re-evaluated in the light of new archaeological data. Oracle-bone inscriptions provide invaluable data on the late Shang dynasty, but little information on earlier periods. Most texts were written hundreds, if not thousands, of years after the Erlitou and early Shang periods. Oral transmission and the court historians who made the records, therefore, inevitably modified these textual accounts.

In addition, modern interpretations of ancient texts may be misleading. For example, it was commonly believed that some late Shang lords and *fang* polities mentioned in the oracle-bone inscriptions were located in southern Shanxi (e.g. Chang 1980: 216-22; Shima 1958: 441; Zheng 1994: fig. 5). Archaeological data, however, provide no evidence of the existence of polities there during the late Shang dynasty; indeed, all of southern Shanxi may have been largely depopulated (see below).

It is clear that recent archaeological information with a refined chronological scale is crucial to any study of the processes of early state formation in China. Based on such recent archaeological evidence as presented in this study, we argue that the earliest states in China may have developed long before the late Shang dynasty, and that political organization during the Erlitou and early Shang periods may not have been the same as that of the late Shang and Zhou dynasties. Furthermore, the development of early states in China was closely related to particular geographical configurations, the distribution and transportation of key resources, and belief systems. All of these variables need to be taken into account in order to create models of the political and economic processes of these early states.

This study employs an interdisciplinary approach, analyzing data derived from archaeology, geology, cultural geography, ethnohistory, and ancient texts, to investigate the development of early states in China. We focus particularly on settlement patterns and political economies in the Erlitou and Erligang periods (*c.* 1900-1400 BC), during which, we argue throughout the book, state-level social organization emerged and developed.

In the following chapters, we will discuss the major factors crucial for the understanding of the processes of state formation in early China. These include the determination of the major social transformations that took place during the Erlitou period; a description of regional ecological settings, including the locations of key resources (copper, tin, lead and salt) and major transport routes; an analysis of regional settlement patterns in relation to the distribution of key resources; an investigation of intra-settlement patterns of primary centres / capital cities and major regional centres; an examination of the relationships between core and periphery as well as between regional centres, in the light of the control and transport of essential natural resources; and an exploration of the level of state monopolization in the production and distribution of major prestige goods – especially bronze ritual vessels – which may have significantly affected the scale of political control. Finally, we will compare our model of state formation in early China to that of the above-mentioned Western theoretical models. Our major objective is to reconstruct the political economy of the early states.

The temporal scope of this book is limited to the Erlitou and Erligang periods, which shared many similarities in social-political organization, and best demonstrate the characteristics of the earliest states in China. The late Shang dynasty (the Anyang phase) is not included in the current research, partly because there may have been a social-political transformation taking place after the Erligang period (see below). A future and separate monograph will be devoted to the study of the new type of social development experienced in the late Shang dynasty.

2

Searching for the Early State in China: Erlitou

Early states: when, where, what, and how

Issues concerning the dates, locations, participants, and developmental processes of the earliest states in China have been at the centre of ongoing debates among archaeologists and historians. Such disputes are the consequence of correlations between certain early Bronze Age cultures (such as Erlitou and Erligang) and historical states named in ancient texts (such as Xia and Shang), and of questions about levels of social complexity within these Bronze Age cultures. Much attention has focused on the Erlitou culture. Because of its spatial and temporal correlation with the Xia dynasty, traditionally believed to be the first dynasty in Chinese history, some archaeologists and historians, especially those whose early education was in China, have come to agree: that the Erlitou culture represents the material remains of at least of part of the Xia dynasty (c. 2100-1600 BC); that the Erlitou site may have been a capital city of the late Xia; and that the Erlitou developed into a state-level society (e.g. Chang 1999: 71-3; Du et al. 1999; Zhao 1987; Zou 1990).

Opinions are divided among scholars about the nature of Erlitou culture. The majority of archaeologists and historians in China agree that Erlitou culture represents a state-level society, and that the Erlitou site represents a capital city of the Xia or Shang dynasties, although they disagree about the identity

26

of the capital city, named in textual records, to which the Erlitou site corresponds. Many Western Sinologists and archaeologists, from a culturally external viewpoint and detached from textual traditions, have challenged all suggestions that there was a historic link between the Xia and Erlitou, and that Erlitou was a state-level society, as discussed in Chapter 1.

The Xia-Shang-Zhou Chronology Project, a state-supported project recently completed in China (Xia Shang Zhou 2000), has stimulated even more scholarly and international public debate about the earliest dynastic history of China. In these debates Chinese archaeologists have been criticized by some Western scholars as being motivated by nationalist agendas and as blindly following ancient textual traditions in their research (Eckholm 2000; Gilley 2000).

It should be noted that, from its birth, modern archaeology in China has never been free from a modern socio-political context (Liu and Chen 2001a). However, it is by no means the case that archaeology in China has been used as an instrument only for assisting politicians to achieve political goals, or that all Chinese archaeologists simple-mindedly manipulate archaeological data in order to support ancient texts. Despite the social-political and financial restraints placed on Chinese intellectuals, archaeologists have produced a great wealth of information through their fieldwork and research during the past few decades, including data from both salvage and historically oriented projects. These data constitute the foundation for further comprehensive analyses (Chang 1981).

It is true, however, that knowledge of the development of early states in ancient China has appeared elusive to the Western world. The language barrier and the employment of different research orientations have been the major factors which make scholarly communication difficult between the East and the West. In addition, scholars from different backgrounds may employ differing definitions of state-level social organization when they examine archaeological evidence from China, although many of them do not explicitly address the criteria that lead to their conclusions.

Archaeological discoveries of several Bronze Age sites during the twentieth century have changed the early dynasties from legendary stories into historic events. Chinese archaeologists have made great efforts to reconstruct the early dynastic history by combining archaeological data with textual information. It may be impossible to detach oneself completely from ancient texts, which in many cases have been enlightening to archaeological investigations and interpretations. It is necessary, however, to treat archaeological information in its own right, to be critical of traditional textual records, and to compare the two sets of data with caution.

Focusing on the political-economic perspective, our discussion is more concerned with questions relating to the levels of social complexity in the early Bronze Age cultures of Erlitou and Erligang, than with issues of historical linkage between Erlitou and the Xia dynasty. Most scholars agree that the Shang civilization originated long before the remains found at Anyang (Yinxu phase), and that Zhengzhou (the Erligang phase) should be regarded as an early part of the Shang dynasty, based on similarities in material culture between Zhengzhou and Anyang.

In spite of the common usage of the term 'Early Shang culture' to refer to material remains dating to the Erligang culture, we will avoid this usage in this book for three reasons. First, not all Chinese archaeologists agree that the Erligang culture represents the early Shang dynasty, since some scholars regard Erlitou as the earliest phase of the Shang (e.g. Henan Institute 2001: 1003-20; Zheng 1983). Secondly, it is debatable whether historic capitals named in traditional texts can be identified with archaeological sites without documentary evidence to support such links (e.g. Bagley 1999; Barnes 1993: 130).

28

Thirdly, the aim of this book is to reconstruct the social formation of the early state, based primarily on archaeological data,
and this objective can be achieved without getting involved in
the debates about ambiguous names and the locations of capitals mentioned in traditional texts. Nevertheless, we provide a
chronological table which illustrates the comparative timelines
of dynastic sequences and archaeological cultures commonly
used in Chinese archaeological literature (Table 2 on p. 11).

Erlitou: the chiefdom or state

The Erlitou culture, centred at the type-site Erlitou in the Yiluo
River basin, has been the focus of attention in the debates
concerning the development of the earliest state in ancient
China. Some 38 calibrated radiocarbon dates derived from Erlitou sites in Henan (Institute of Archaeology 1991) and results
from the recently accomplished 'Xia-Shang-Zhou Chronology
Project' (Xia Shang Zhou 2000) indicate that this culture may
have flourished between 1900 and 1500 BC. The Erlitou period
is further divided into four successive phases based on changes
in ceramic styles, each estimated at around 100 years (Institute
of Archaeology 1999: 392). Erlitou, at 300 hectares in area
(Erlitou 2001), is the largest of all contemporary sites in China,
and sites containing Erlitou material assemblages have been
found over a very broad region, mainly including Henan, southern Shanxi, Eastern Shaanxi, and Hubei (Figure 1).

Several marked changes in settlement pattern and material
culture took place when the Longshan culture of the late Neolithic period developed into the Erlitou culture:

Settlement hierarchy in western and central Henan changed
from two- or three-tiered systems in the late Longshan period
to a four-tiered system in the Erlitou culture (Figure 2) and
rank-size curves changed from convex to strong primate (Fig-

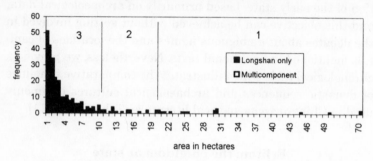

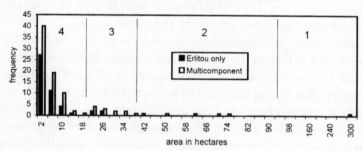

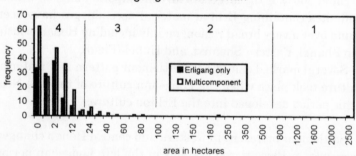

Figure 2. Histograms showing settlement hierarchy changing from three-tiered in the late Longshan culture to four-tiered in the Erlitou and Erligang periods.

2. Searching for the Early State in China: Erlitou

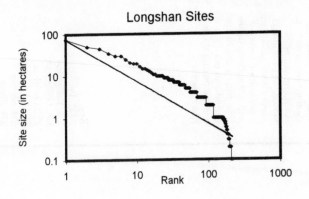

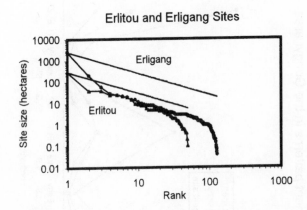

Figure 3. Rank-size curves showing convex during the late Longshan period in Henan changing to strong primate in the Erlitou and Erligang periods.

ure 3). All these measurements point to the development of centralized political and economic control (Liu 1996b, 2000).[1]

The political structure of a regional level changed from the coexistence of multiple competing polities into one in which a single large centre dominated smaller centres and villages over a very broad area (Liu 1996b, 2000).

Settlement nucleation took place in the Yiluo region, as Erlitou sites were densely distributed in the region (Chen *et al.*

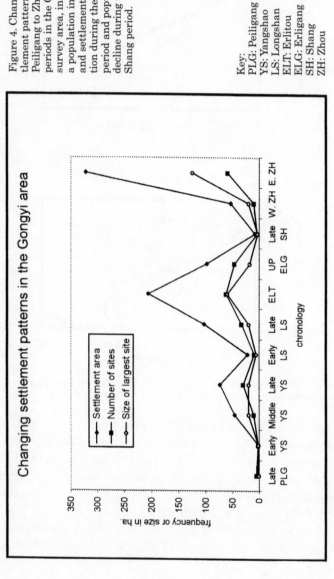

Figure 4. Changing settlement patterns from Peiligang to Zhou periods in the Gongyi survey area, indicating a population increase and settlement nucleation during the Erlitou period and population decline during the late Shang period.

Key:
PLG: Peiligang
YS: Yangshao
LS: Longshan
ELT: Erlitou
ELG: Erligang
SH: Shang
ZH: Zhou

2003) and the largest site size increased from no more than 40 ha in the Longshan period (Zhao 2001: 144) to 300 ha in the Erlitou period. These changes suggest nucleation of population accompanying urbanism (Liu 1996b, forthcoming). Such nucleation is especially evident in the core area of the urbanism, the Yiluo basin, where several secondary centres clustered with small settlements developed in close proximity to Erlitou (Figure 1). The recent data from systematic surveys in the Gongyi area, the eastern part of the Yiluo basin, suggest that this area experienced a population decline from late Longshan to Erlitou Phase I and then a population increase along with settlement nucleation in Erlitou Phases II and III (Figure 4) (Chen *et al.* 2003).

Ceramic styles changed from diversity (six variants of the Longshan culture in Henan and southern Shanxi) to relative uniformity (two variants of the Erlitou culture, Erlitou and Dongxiafeng, in the same region). This may suggest an increase in the specialization and standardization of craft production relating to the development of political centralization (cf. Longacre 1999; Rice 1981, 1996).

In addition to jade objects and finely made ceramics such as white pottery vessels, which were the traditional means for representing high social ranking in the Neolithic, bronze objects, mainly weapons and ritual vessels, became status symbols for the first time. Bronze production, which was largely based at Erlitou, appears to have become closely associated with state affairs, especially for military and ritual use (Liu 2003).

Long-distance exchange of precious goods developed to a new level – some cowries (*Monetaria moneta* or *Monetaria annulus*) with possible origins in the Indian Ocean region (Peng and Zhu 1999) were added to the inventory of grave goods in elite burials. Some artifacts and decorative motifs with characteristics of Central Asian cultures also appeared at Erlitou (Fitzgerald-Huber 1995).

Most importantly, the Erlitou site itself developed into a highly stratified urban centre, characterized by polarization between rich and poor burials, the construction of a large temple/palace complex, and by the concentration of population who were involved in various specialized craft productions including bronze, bone, and ceramics (Institute of Archaeology 1999; Liu forthcoming) (more details below).

Some of the phenomena listed above can be observed in some archaeological cultures during the late Neolithic period, including social stratification manifested in mortuary remains, long-distance exchange of elite goods (Liu 1996a), and hierarchically organized settlement systems (Liu 1996b). However, the degree of complexity in those Neolithic societies was lower than that of Erlitou, and all the above-mentioned variables did not occur all together at any single Neolithic site. Furthermore, those Neolithic societies seem to have gone through cycles alternating between development and decline, which is a phenomenon commonly characteristic of chiefdoms (see Wright 1977). For the first time and during the Erlitou period, dramatic changes occurred across the entire social system. These changes signify the emergence of a new social formation, the state, which was much more integrated economically and centralized politically at the regional level than ever before.

A state is defined in this study as a society with a minimum of two strata, a professional ruling class and a commoner class. The ruling class is characterized by a centralized decision-making process, which is both externally specialized, with regard to the local processes which it regulates, and internally specialized in that the central process is divisible into separate activities which can be performed in different places at different times (see Marcus and Feinman 1998: 4; Wright 1977: 383). Furthermore, a state-level social organization often develops a four- or more tiered regional settlement hierarchy, which implies three or more levels of administrative hierarchy (e.g. Earle 1991: 3; Flannery 1998: 16-21; Wright 1977: 389; Wright and Johnson 1975). These criteria will be used to examine the nature of the Erlitou culture in the following chapters.

The establishment of a major centre at Erlitou may have involved many political, economic, and environmental factors. The Yiluo River valley is a vast fertile alluvial basin, surrounded by the Yellow River and the Mangling Hills to the north, and mountain ranges on the other three sides. The Yi and Luo Rivers flow from west to east through the basin and join together forming a single river channel before emptying into the Yellow River. The fertile alluvial land in the basin insured high yields of agricultural products, such as grains and domesticated animals, supporting a high population density. The environmentally circumscribed condition of the basin apparently had advantages for its military defensibility, which may partially account for the lack of a city wall at the major centre. However, the Yiluo basin had its disadvantages: the lack of non-agricultural natural resources.

Several types of resources seem to be the most crucial: a large quantity of timber for constructing palaces and temples at Erlitou; lithic materials for making stone tools; kaolin clay for making elite ceramics (white pottery); copper, tin, and lead for casting bronzes; timber and charcoal as fuel for casting bronzes; and salt for cooking and processing food. Most of these items cannot now be found, and could not be found, at least in sufficient quantities, in ancient times, on the alluvial plains near Erlitou; but they were available from surrounding regions within a ratio distance of 20-200 km from Erlitou. In order to understand the economic-political operation of the early state, it is crucial to investigate where and how Erlitou obtained and transported these resources.

3

The Natural Landscape: Resources and Transport Routes

The development of urbanism required a constant flow of vital resources to the primary centre. Erlitou was located on a central axis of communication routes in all directions, either by river or on land, which lead to the areas where natural resources occurred in abundance. Many secondary centres distributed throughout the region facilitated the procurement and transportation of these resources (Figure 1). The spatial distribution of these resources, major communication routes, and the location of secondary regional centres, therefore, determined the early state's political-economic activities and its ability to control and transport these resources.

Distribution of key resources

The early state procured key resources in areas both close to and far from Erlitou. Stone sources were distributed in the Songshan Mountains and Mangling Hills (Gongxian 1991; Yanshi 1992), Kaolin deposits were available on the outskirts of the Yiluo basin where porcelain kilns of later historical times have been found (Yang 1991b: 44-6); a large quantity and good quality of timber were also available in the mountainous regions surrounding the Yiluo basin, and charcoal making was one of the traditional industries in the highland areas in Gongyi prior

36

to the 1920s (Gongxian 1989: 91, 107). However, metal and salt had to be obtained from much further away. Our focus will be on the latter two types of resource, which were most closely related to the development of early states. As these resources occurred in high concentrations only in a few locations, they became important strategic materials which needed to be controlled by the state. The procurement of these resources, as we will demonstrate later, affected the settlement patterns and territorial expansion of early states.

Metals

Bronze objects of the Erlitou and Shang periods were made of alloys that included copper, tin, and lead. Bronze vessels dating from the Erlitou to the Shang periods increased gradually in size, weight, and quantity, suggesting an increase in the control of resources and in the supplies of copper, tin, and lead through time.

According to modern geological investigations, copper mines are distributed broadly but unevenly across regions in China, with total deposits of 73 million tons. While the majority of areas only have moderate quantities of copper ore, four regions possess two-thirds of China's copper deposits. These include copper zones in the middle and lower Yangzi River valley, the Dongchuan and Yimen mines in Yunnan, the Zhongtiao mountain mines in southern Shanxi, and the Baiyinchang and Jinchuan mines in Gansu (Hua 1999: 48-9; Zhu 1999: 182-90). Most of these mining areas were explored in antiquity, after the surface layers of the deposits were exhausted. In addition, many more copper deposits, probably mined in ancient times, were recorded in early texts. According to Shih Chang-ju (Shih 1955), such deposits were found in many regions of China (Figure 5).

Tin mines are concentrated in only few areas in China, with

37

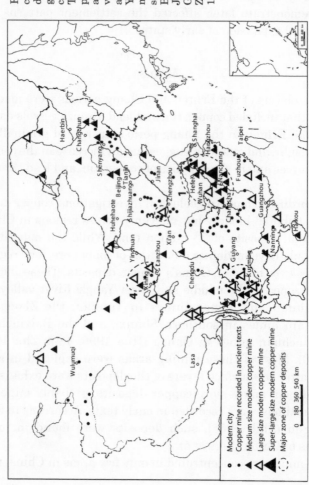

Figure 5. Distribution of copper deposits in China, determined by modern geological surveys and recorded in ancient texts. There are four major copper zones: 1 the middle and lower Yangzi River valley; 2 the Dongchuan and Yimen mines in Yunnan; 3 the Zhongtiao mountains mines in southern Shanxi; 4 the Baiyinchang and Jinchuan mines in Gansu (redrawn from Zhu 1999:188; Shih 1955: fig. 1).

a total deposit of 5.6 million tons. Although some fifteen provinces are reported to have tin; six of them – including Yunnan, Guangxi, Guangdong, Hunan, Inner Mongolia, and Jiangxi – possess 97.7% of the total deposits (Zhu 1999: 381-403). It is apparent that northern China is tin-poor, as most tin deposits occur to the south of the Yangzi River. According to modern geological surveys, the medium-sized tin mine closest to the Central Plains is located in De'an, Jiangxi. From textual records, however, Shih Chang-ju has identified some seventeen locations associated with tin deposits around the Central Plains, including Henan, Hebei, Shanxi, and Shandong (Shih 1955) (Figure 6). It is conceivable that some small tin mines existed in the Yellow River valley and were exploited during the early dynastic period, but that most of them were exhausted in antiquity.

Lead is also widely distributed over China. Some 732 lead mines with a total deposit of 41 million tons, had been located by the end of 1996. About 64% of China's entire lead deposits today are concentrated in a few regions in Yunnan, Inner Mongolia, Gansu, Guangdong, Hunan, and Guangxi (Zhu 1999: 238-48) (Figure 7). Lead ingots have been discovered in bronze foundries at Zhengzhou (Henan Institute 1989b: 118) and at Anyang (Chen 1991), suggesting that lead was brought separately into the major centres for casting processes during these periods. Opinions on the locations of lead resources vary among scholars. Some specialists have argued that lead deposits were available in the Central Plains and were explored in ancient times, since at least six lead deposits were mined in Henan and Shaanxi during the Northern Song dynasty (AD 960-1127) according to textual records (Figure 7). The Shang people, therefore, may have obtained lead primarily from locations near the core area (Chen 1991). Other scholars are of the opinion that lead sources were located in areas more remote from the core during the Shang period. Lead isotopic analyses on several

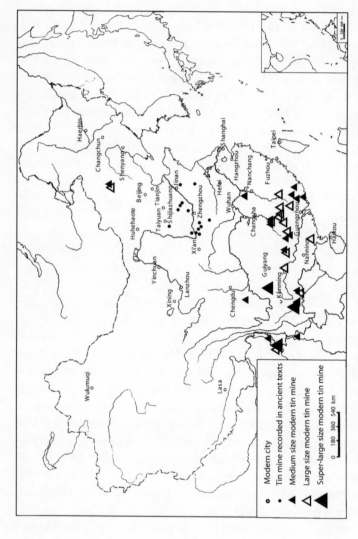

Figure 6. Distribution of tin deposits in China, determined by modern geological surveys and recorded in ancient texts (redrawn from Zhu 1999: 387; Shih 1955: fig.1).

Legend:

○ Modern city
● Tin mine recorded in ancient texts
▲ Medium size modern tin mine
△ Large size modern tin mine
▲ Super-large size modern tin mine

0   180   360   540 km

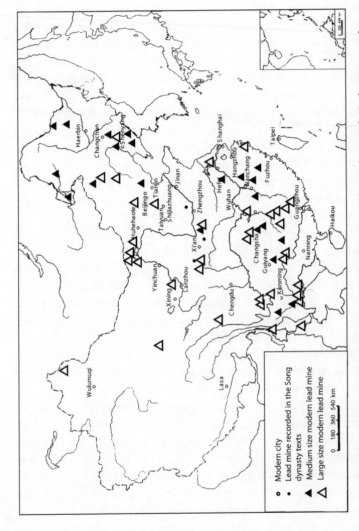

Figure 7. Distribution of lead deposits in China, determined by modern geological surveys and recorded in the Song dynasty texts (redrawn from Zhu 1999: 239; Chen 1991: table 4).

41

bronzes of the early Shang period discovered at Zhengzhou and Yanshi in Henan and at Panlongcheng in Hubei, suggest that these bronzes were made of an unusual type of highly radiogenic lead (Jin *et al.* 1998). The same type of lead has also been identified in the bronzes discovered at Dayangzhou in Jiangxi (Jin *et al.* 1994) and at Sanxingdui in Sichuan (Jin *et al.* 1995), all dated to the late Shang. The exact provenance of this type of lead has not been identified, but it may have related to some highly radiogenic lead deposits in eastern Yunnan and western Guizhou (Jin *et al.* 1994, 1995). These phenomena suggest that direct or indirect communication or contact between the Central Plains and periphery during the Shang dynasty may have reached areas much further south than previously thought, and that both local and non-local lead sources may have been obtained during the early dynastic period.

Among these major ore deposits, two areas seem to have been within the reach of the Erlitou and Erligang cultural distribution: the Zhongtiao Mountains in southern Shanxi and the middle and lower Yangzi River valley, as indicated by the distribution of Erlitou and Erligang material remains in these regions. The copper deposits in these two regions may have been among the earliest to be exploited.

The Zhongtiao Mountains possess one of the major copper deposits in China. Among about 100 large and medium sized copper mines in the country, five are located in the Zhongtiao Mountains with total copper deposits of about 340,000 tons.[1] According to local archaeologists, there were many small, shallow mines, referred to as *jiwokuang* (chicken-nest mines), which would have been exhausted quickly by local miners. These mines were probably oxidized ore deposits which occur on the surface level, and many such mines may have been worked out in antiquity since early mining activities before the Western Zhou were focused on only oxidized copper ores.[2] Archaeologists have found remains of mining activities as well as cord-marked pottery dated to the Erlitou and Shang period at Dahangou, about 7 km west of the Yuanqu town (Tong 1998: 96). Some ancient mines dated to the Eastern Zhou and Eastern Han have been discovered in Yuncheng and Yuanqu respectively (An and Chen 1962; Li 1993). It is important to note that the copper ores mined in the Eastern Zhou have been determined to be sulphide ores (Li 1993).

The copper zones located in the middle and lower Yangzi River valley possess the largest copper deposits in China.[3] Most deposits occur on the surface or are shallowly buried, and the layers of oxidized secondary enrichment deposits are very rich, measuring up to 100 m in thickness at some locations (Golas 1999: 58-69; Hua 1999: 49). These conditions were extremely suitable for ancient mining and smelting techniques. The best-preserved ancient smelting foundries have been found at Tonglushan in Hubei. In an area of 2 km², seven open mining sites, ten underground mining sites, and eight shaft furnaces associated with oxidized copper ores have been found. Mining activities may have started as early as the Shang period and continued to the Western Han period (206 BC – AD 8) (Huangshi 1981, 1999) (see below). These findings suggest that there was a long period of utilization of oxidized ores in the middle Yangzi River valley.

Excavations at Tongling in Jiangxi have revealed ancient copper mining sites, including a mining area of 7 ha, three smelting areas totalling 17.6 ha, and the remains of three miners' shelters made of wood, bamboo and reed mats. Archaeologists have found large quantities of slag estimated at about 300,000 tons near the smelting areas. Ancient miners exploited the mines at Tongling in Ruichang, Jiangxi, from the Upper Erligang to the early Eastern Zhou period (*c.* fourteenth to fifth century BC), and undertook mining activities there on a large scale during the Shang dynasty. Some 41 mining shafts are dated to the Shang period, constituting 47.5% of the shafts

43

found at the site. Some 128 artifacts, including wooden and bronze tools and ceramic utensils, are also dated to the Shang period (Liu and Lu 1997). Shang miners seem to have employed methods combining surface and shallow underground mining to exploit the area with the richest ore deposits (Lu and Liu 1997).

Copper mining activities at Tonglushan in Daye, Hubei, may have taken place in the Yinxu period, based on ^{14}C dates of wooden samples from mining shafts (Institute of Archaeology 1991: 192-3). The beginning of exploitation of copper in the Daye region may have started even earlier, however, as copper smelting sites dated to the Erligang period have been found at Mianyangdi, Gutangdun, and Lihe in Daye, all located in close proximity to copper mines in the region (Huangshi 1984).

The distribution of oxidized copper deposits is important to the understanding of mining activities in early Chinese civilization. Such deposits probably existed in many locations in relatively small quantities, but occurred in especially high concentrations in the lower and middle Yangzi River valley. This factor, as discussed below, had considerable impact on the strategies of copper procurement during the Erlitou and Shang periods.

Since the archaeological record provides us with greater evidence and knowledge of the procurement of copper than of tin and lead by early states, and copper is the major component in bronze alloys, the discussion of metal resources in this book focuses primarily on copper procurement and metallurgy.

Salt

Salt is an important component in the human diet (Denton 1982), and can be used in other types of subsistence production, such as hide processing (Potts 1984). Consequently salt production often played an important role in the development of the economic systems of ancient civilizations, including those of China (Adshead 1992). A single large salt resource, the Hedong

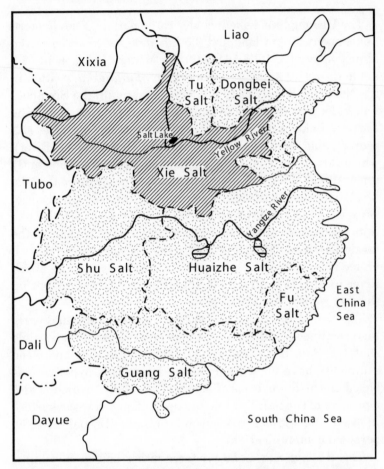

Figure 8. Location of the Hedong Salt Lake and the distribution area of Hedong salt (Xie salt) in the Song dynasty (redrawn from Guo 1997: 270).

Salt Lake in the Yuncheng basin, southern Shanxi, was the major salt supply (known as Xie salt) for a large region in the middle Yellow River valley and a part of the Huai River valley (Figure 8). This is the region where earliest urbanization developed, and the Hedong Salt Lake may thus have been essential to the economy of early states.

45

The Hedong Salt Lake includes three parts: (1) the Eastern Lake, about 25 km long and 3.5 km wide, as recorded in the Ming dynasty (AD 1368-1644); (2) the Western Lake, about 12.5 km long and 10 km wide, according to *Shuijingzhu*, written in the Northern Wei dynasty (AD 386-534); and (3) the Six Small Lakes, located near the Western Lake (Chai 1991: 1-5). The Eastern Lake was the major salt production site. The salt source came from a brine stream, the Heihe (Black River), which flowed through the site. The Salt Lake was constantly under threat of flood from the surrounding areas, since the lake is relatively low in the basin. In antiquity, rammed-earth enclosures were built and rebuilt repeatedly to protect the Salt Lake from floods, and canal systems were constructed to channel the floodwater away from the Salt Lake area. In spite of such protections, sediments carried by a flood blocked the Black River in AD 1757. After that, the brine had to be brought up through wells (Chai 1991: 78-85).

The size of the Salt Lake system in prehistoric and early historic times is unknown, but may have varied. It is possible that the Salt Lake was larger than at present, and flood sediments have buried part of the Lake. This hypothesis is based on the discoveries of layers of mirabilite, which is also a product of the Salt Lake, found up to 12 m below the surface in areas a few kilometres beyond the Lake (Li, Baiqin 1999, personal communication).

The Hedong Salt Lake produces either salt or mirabilite, depending on the preparation of the brine in different seasons, but salt seems to have been the major product in antiquity. Because of its high mirabilite content, Hedong salt tasted bitter. Hedong salt was made by a solar-evaporation process. According to text records, the earliest salt production relied on summer wind and solar heat for drying up the brine in the field, and the salt harvest took place around August and September each year. Beginning in the Tang dynasty (AD 618-907), at the

46

latest, paddy-field techniques were employed. This method required a long period of preparation. Beginning in February, artificial paddy fields were made; from April on, the brine was channelled into the paddies and mixed with a certain amount of fresh water in order to produce high quality salt; then, in August, the strong summer wind and solar heat turned the brine into salt within 4-5 days and the salt was harvested (Chai 1991). The production process may have been very labour-intensive and highly seasonal, as salt harvesting was concentrated over a very short period. Productivity may have been unstable before the introduction of the paddy-field techniques in the Tang dynasty, prior to which productivity was affected if precipitation was too high during the harvesting season.

Hedong salt is in the form of crystals; the larger the size of the salt crystals, the better its quality (Guo 1997: 110). Salt was used as a ritual offering in the Western Zhou dynasty (1045-771 BC) (Sun 1987: 411-12), and was a major source of state revenue throughout the dynastic eras (Chai 1991: 31-50). The many legends associated with the Hedong Salt Lake (Chai 1991: 6-17) hint at its cultural and economic significance in ancient times. Since Hedong salt was formed naturally and was easy to collect, it may have been one of the earliest salt resources utilized by people long before historic times.

Sources of salt for the lower Yellow River region were mainly in the Bohai Bay area, where seawater was boiled down to make salt in antiquity. A type of ceramic, referred to as *kuixingqi* (helmet-shaped vessels) and dated to the late Shang dynasty, has been found at many sites near the coast. Such vessels have very thick walls with curved or pointed bases. The exterior was decorated with thick cord-marks, and traces of burning on the exterior surface are often visible, suggesting that these vessels may have been used for boiling seawater to make salt (Shandong Institute 1989: 180). These vessels have been found in small quantities near the southern and western coasts of the

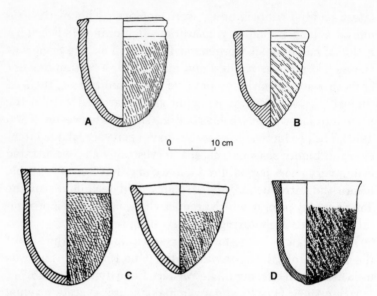

Figure 9. Examples of *kuixingqi* pots (helmet-shaped vessels) used for salt production in late Shang, from coastal areas in the Bohai Bay. A and **B**: from kiln sites near Lijin (after Wang et al. 1997: figs 3.2; 4.1); **C**: from Fenghuang-tai in Qingzhou (after Shandong Institute 1989: fig. 20:10, 11); **D**: from Zhaopu in Qingzhou (after Xia 1989: fig. 11:2).

Bohai Bay in northern Shandong, such as Dinggong in Zouping (Shandong University 1992: 503), Fenghuangtai in Qingzhou (Shandong Institute 1989: 163), and Zhaopu in Qingzhou (Xia 1989: 195). The largest finds have been made at four large pottery kiln sites near Lijin, which may have specialized in making such vessels for the salt production taking place nearby (Liu and Chen 2000, 2001b; Wang *et al.* 1997) (Figure 9). These *kuixingqi* vessels also show some characteristics of the indigenous cultural tradition from the Yueshi culture (an archaeological culture distributed in Shandong and contemporaneous with the Erlitou culture), in terms of their ceramic form (Shandong Institute 1989: 180), suggesting that salt boiling

48

may have been a traditional technique employed by people in the coastal areas long before the Shang dynasty.

The character *lu*, salt, repeatedly occurs in oracle-bone inscriptions as an item desired by the Shang kings (Yang 1992: 634). There were officials appointed by the late Shang court to be in charge of salt management. This is indicated by a passage in the oracle-bone inscriptions, '*lu xiaochen qi you yi*' (Guo 1978-82: fig. 5596), meaning that the salt manager (*lu xiaochen*) possesses a town or settlements with land (*you yi*). Scholars have provided at least nine interpretations for the term *xiaochen*, which occurs in different contexts in oracle-bone inscriptions, ranging from high officials to slaves, as Zhou (2000) summarized. According to recent research, *xiaochen* may have referred to the officials who originated from non-Shang lineages, or were promoted from lower statuses but served the Shang court (Wang 2002; Zhou 2000).

It is not clear from the inscriptions whether salt was obtained by the Shang kings as a tributary item or as a product of industry controlled by the late Shang royal court. Considering the evidence for the large scale of salt production found near Lijin, an area within the distribution of late Shang material culture, it is conceivable that, to some extent, the salt industry was under the direct management of the late Shang state. If this was the case, a state-controlled salt industry long predated Guan Zhong (*c.* 685 BC) of the Qi state in northern Shandong, who, according to text records, brought prosperity to the Qi by making salt distribution and trade a state monopoly (Guo 1997: 26-30).

Throughout most of the dynastic period in China, salt was one of the most important commodities controlled by states, and its production, transportation, and distribution were highly regulated (Guo 1997). It is possible that early forms of such control may have originated at the very beginning of state formation.

State Formation in Early China

Major communication routes

How raw material resources were transported from the periphery to the core is another crucial factor which affected urban
development. We will continue to focus on two regions – the
lower and middle Yangzi River valley and southern Shanxi –
where bronze alloys and salt needed to be transported to primary centres. As archaeological information is limited on this
subject, we have to rely to some extent on textual data.

Jindao xihang – copper and tin routes

Water transport routes were essential in ancient China (Skinner 1977). Archaeologists have found wooden paddles and rud-
ders at Chengtoushan in Hunan (*c.* 5000-3000 BC) (He 1994a;
Hunan Institute 1999: 17-30) and Hemudu in Zhejiang (*c.* 5000-
3400 BC) (Hemudu 1980: 6), so that boats, as a means of transportation, can be traced back to the Neolithic period in southern
China. It is important to note that several major river courses
in the early dynastic period were different from the way they
are now. These include the Yellow River before the Western
Zhou, which turned northeast near Wuzhi in Henan, flowed
through the Hebei plains, and finally emptied into the Bohai
Bay near Tianjin (Tan 1981; 1982: 17-18); and the Ji River, an
ancient branch of the Yellow River which disappeared in later
times, which flowed in a similar course to the present Yellow
River's lower course and the course of the Xiaoqing River. And a
third river, the Si in Shandong, connected the Huai River in the
south to the Ji River through Lake Heze in the north (Tan 1982:
17-18, 20-1). These rivers were important communication routes
connecting the Central Plains with the surrounding regions. Evidence from ancient texts and bronze inscriptions, as we shall see
below, suggests that at least three major routes may have been used
to link the lower and middle Yangzi River valley with the core area

50

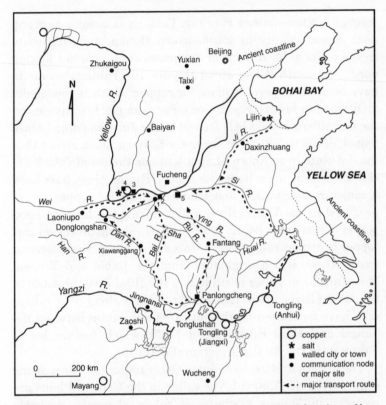

Figure 10. Locations of river channels in early dynastic times; locations of key natural resources; major transportation routes with communication nodes linking primary centres in the core area with the middle and lower Yangzi River valley in the south, the Wei River in the west, and the coastal region in the east (1: Erlitou, 2: Yanshi, 3: Yuanqu, 4: Dongxiafeng, 5: Zhengzhou).

in the north. We will refer to these as the central, eastern, and western routes for the purposes of this discussion (Figure 10).

The central route. In a ninety-word inscription on the Zengbo Qi *fu* bronze vessel dated to the Eastern Zhou period (770-476 BC), it is mentioned that the Zhou opened a route for copper and tin, *jindao xihang*, in order to obtain metal ingots from Huaiyi in the lower Yangzi River valley, and that the route passed through a place named Fantang. Fantang is today's Fanyang near Xincai county in southeastern Henan, and this route seems to have been a major communication channel linking north and south (Chen 1995) (Figure 10). Fantang seems to have been an important place for copper, which is repeatedly mentioned in bronze inscriptions. For example, inscriptions on the Rongsheng bronze bell-set and on the Jin Jiang *ding* bronze tripod, dated to 740 BC in the early Eastern Zhou, record that the Jin state in southern Shanxi sent one thousand vehicles of salt to Fantang to exchange for copper. Fantang may have been a major redistribution and trading centre for copper ingots produced in the Yangzi River valley during the Eastern Zhou period (Chen 1995: 34; Li 1999), and its establishment on this copper transport route may be traced to earlier periods. Several small rivers, which originated from the Dabie and Tongbai Mountains, run either north to join the Huai River or south to the Yangzi River. These rivers and the roads along river valleys may have facilitated north-south communication between the Yangzi and Huai Rivers (Song 1983), which further led to Fantang via the Ru River system (Figure 10).

The eastern and western routes. Other routes for transporting copper from the Yangzi River valley to the Central Plains are recorded in 'Yugong' (Tributes of Yu) in *Shangshu*, probably compiled during the Eastern Zhou period (Jin and Lu 1996: 285-8). Two regions providing metal as tribute to the capital cities in the Central Plains were Yangzhou and Jingzhou, refer-ring to regions in the lower and middle Yangzi River valley, respectively. The two communication routes were as the follows: in the east, tribute from Yangzhou was transported on the Yangzi, Huai, and Si Rivers, through the Ji and Yellow Rivers to the primary centres; in the west, tribute from Jingzhou was carried on the Yangzi, Han, Dan, Luo, and Yellow Rivers to the core (Chen 1995) (Figure 10).

Some Erlitou and Erligang sites have been discovered along

the western routes. At the Jingnansi site near Jingzhou in Hubei, ceramic assemblages primarily resemble those of Erlitou Phases II and IV and early Shang dynasty, while some hardware ceramics and protoporcelain with stamped geometric patterns point to origins in the middle Yangzi River valley (Jingzhou Museum 1989). The site had easy access to the Yangzi River, and the coexistence of a mix of cultural elements there suggests regional interactions between north and south. At Xiawanggang near Xichuan in southwestern Henan, Erlitou cultural remains are dated to Phase I and III, and a hardware ceramic jar decorated with stamped geometric patterns dating to Erlitou Phase I was discovered there (Henan Institute 1989a). This jar, which had a southern origin, marks the earliest occurrence of such hardware in the Henan region (Peng 1987: 344-7). Xiawanggang, located near the Dan River, was situated along the western transport route (Figure 10). In addition, several early Shang sites have been found along the middle Yangzi River (He 1994b: fig. 1), which may have also functioned as transportation nodes (see Figure 24 on p. 107). The locations of these sites and the mixed southern and northern cultural characteristics seem to support the ancient texts, suggesting that communications between the core area in the Yellow River region and the middle Yangzi River valley may have been facilitated by these river courses as early as the Erlitou period.

There may have been more than one communication channel used in antiquity along the western routes. It was also possible to travel along the Han River and the Bai River into the Nanyang basin, Henan, and then go northward along the Ya River, passing the Luyang Pass, crossing the watershead in the Funiu Mountains, and continuing along the Sha River system to Lushan and Linru, finally reaching the Yiluo basin. This way was the major communication route between the Yangzi-Han River system and the Central Plains through the Nanyang basin in historical times (Wang 1996). Many Shang sites have been found in the Nanyang basin and along the Sha River system, suggesting that these routes may have been utilized during the Shang period (Figure 10).

The tributary goods from the south, mentioned in 'Yugong', were not limited to metals, but may have included many other valuables such as ivory, feathers, leather, turtle shells, protoporcelain, etc., and both river and land roads may have been used as communication routes (Chen 1995: 333). Judging from the distances involved, the central route seems to have been the most efficient one if the destination were Zhengzhou, while the western routes may have been the best for Erlitou.

Salt routes

The best-recorded information on Hedong salt transportation is from the Qing dynasty (AD 1644-1911). There were three major routes for transporting salt to the surrounding areas. Through the western route, the salt was carried on land roads to the port of Jiamakou on the Yellow River, then shipped by boat on the Yellow and Wei Rivers to the Shaanxi region. By the southeastern route, salt was carried across the Zhongtiao Mountains in Pinglu county, and shipped across the Yellow River through the port of Maojindu, leading to further transport in Henan. Through the northern route, salt was transported through Xiaxian, Wenxi and Jiangxian, and further redistributed in northern Shanxi and Hebei (Chai 1991: 46, 55; Figure 11). Among these routes, the southern one through Pinglu was the most difficult one, as the road was mostly in steep mountain areas (Wei 1998: 194). These routes may not have been exactly the same in early historic times, and an eastern route also seems to have been used in antiquity.

The existence of this eastern route is indicated by the inscriptions on a stone weight made in AD 1092 (Northern Song), the *Yuanquxian dianxiayang* (the weight of Yuanqu county) dis-

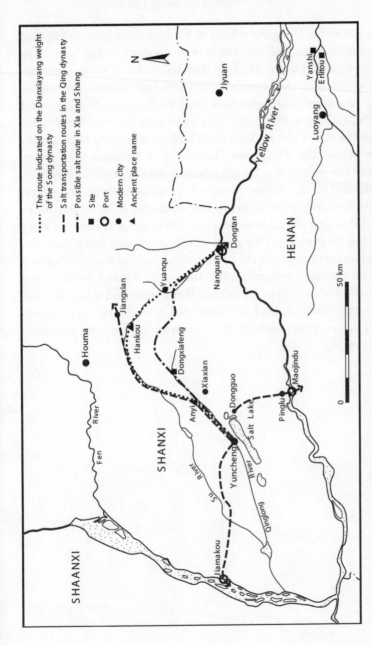

Figure 11. Ancient salt routes in southern Shanxi, through which Hedong salt was transported to the surrounding regions.

55

covered at the Dongtan village in Yuanqu (Guo 1987; Wang and Lu 1986). This 140 kg stone was used to weigh salt bags transported from the Hedong Salt Lake. Based on the inscriptions carved on the stone weight, three such objects were made and placed at transportation stations in Anyi, Hankou, and Yuanqu along a salt road. This road took the northern route from the Salt Lake to Anyi and Hankou, and then went southeast across the Zhongtiao Mountains to Dongtan in Yuanqu where the weight was found. Dongtan was near an ancient port (Jimindu) on the Yellow River, where salt bags were loaded on boats for further transport to the southeast (Chai 1991: 56) in the Yiluo and Zhengzhou regions, where ancient capitals were located (Figure 11). This eastern salt route may have been the most important one in the period of the early states (see below).

The communication routes were not limited to the ones described above. The Yellow and Wei Rivers and many of their tributaries would also have been used as major transport channels connecting eastern and western regions in antiquity (Figure 10).

4

The Erlitou State: Centralization and Territorial Expansion

The most striking characteristics of the Erlitou period are the rapid expansion of Erlitou material culture to neighbouring regions, and increasing stratification within the social system of political centres. The mechanism governing the political system and the dynamics underlying social changes can be understood by analyzing intra-site settlement patterns at Erlitou and inter-regional relationships, both between regional centres on different levels of settlement hierarchy, and across the region where Erlitou sites are distributed.

Erlitou: the major centre

Excavations at Erlitou since 1959 have yielded abundant material remains including large architectural foundations, bronze-casting and bone-carving workshops, pottery kilns, house foundations, burials of different social status, bronze and jade ritual objects, and enormous amounts of stone, bone, shell, and pottery artifacts (Erlitou 1983a, 1983b, 1984, 1985, 1992; Institute of Archaeology 1999).

Erlitou was first occupied by small groups of Neolithic settlers in the middle Yangshao (c. 4000-3500 BC) and early Longshan (c. 3000-2500 BC) periods, and then developed into a large urban site during the Erlitou period. In Erlitou Phase I

57

the site appears to have become a sizeable settlement, probably a regional centre, whose actual site size has yet to be determined. It was associated with several types of craft production, making bronze, pottery and bone artifacts. Since there was a 500-year gap between Neolithic and Erlitou occupations, Erlitou's initial development toward urbanism was unlikely to have been a process of natural population growth at the site, but rather the result of migration of population from elsewhere. The process of urbanization began in Phase II, reached its peak in Phase III, and declined in Phase IV (*c.* 1800-1500 BC). By the Erligang period (*c.* 1500-1400 BC), the site had become a small village before being completely abandoned (Institute of Archaeology 1999; Liu forthcoming).

During the peak of its development (Phase III), Erlitou appears to be partitioned into several sections with specialized functions. Archaeologists found a palatial zone, about 7.5 ha in area in the centre of the site, indicated by a few dozen rammed-earth foundations (ranging in area between 600 m^2 to 1 ha), among which the two largest ones (Palaces no. 1 and no. 2) have been excavated. Palace no. 1 (1 ha) comprised a rammed-earth terrace as the palace foundation (9585 m^2), on which a single edifice was reconstructed; walls with roofed galleries enclosed this structure with a large front courtyard. The rammed-earth foundation was more than 3 m thick, and three layers of pebbles (50 x 30 m in area and 60-65 cm thick) were placed on the lower level of the foundation (Institute of Archaeology 1999: 138-44). It should be noted that pebbles do not exist in the Luo River near the site today, and this situation was probably the same in ancient times. Such a large quantity of pebbles found in the palace area, therefore, would have been obtained from rivers near mountainous regions. A smaller structure, Palace no. 2 (4200 m^2), located 150 m northeast of Palace no. 1, comprised a rectangular-shaped rammed-earth foundation (about 1070 m^2), supporting the main structure, which was divided by wattle-

and-daub walls into three rooms. A square-shaped pit, which the excavators suggested was a large looted tomb, was located in the area between the rammed-earth platform and the northern wall.[1] Walls with attached galleries then enclosed the eastern, southern and western sides of compound, and two small houses were located on the eastern and western sides (Institute of Archaeology 1999: 151-9; Thorp 1991). Several scholars have interpreted these buildings as palaces or temples (e.g. Yang 2001: 26-42; Zou 1979: 24-8), or as settings for ceremonial performances watched by an audience of several thousand (Bagley 1999: 160). Although the exact functions of these buildings are still a matter for speculation, based on differences in size and form, they may have served different functions.

The construction of these buildings must have required earth-moving on a large scale. Zou Heng has estimated that the volume of the rammed-earth foundation of Palace no. 1 was about 20,000 m³, which required more than 100,000 day/man power to construct (Zou 1979: 28). A ditch measuring 8-16 m wide, up to 4 m deep, and more than 350 m long has been found in the eastern border of the site. It was composed of numerous large pits dating from Phase II to Phase IV. Archaeologists have suggested that the soil was removed from these pits for constructing buildings or making pottery at the site (Erlitou 2001).

On the south of the site, an area of 1 ha was occupied by a bronze foundry dating to Phases II-IV, indicated by thick deposits of slag, remains of crucibles, clay moulds, and remains of casting. Kilns and remains of bone manufacture were also found in this area, but the kilns may relate to bronze production, probably for firing clay moulds. It is important to note that the clay moulds found in the bronze foundry included those used for casting tools, weapons, and ritual vessels. Some moulds were used for making very large vessels (up to 36 cm in rim diameter), and others for making vessels of various shapes and elaborate decoration. The equivalent bronze vessels have not been discovered, probably because only medium and small Erlitou tombs have been found to date.[2] These moulds, however, indicate that the Erlitou bronzes may have been much more spectacular than the ones actually found so far (Zheng 1998: 191).

Bone workshops were located both north and east of the site, as indicated by abundant concentrations of grinding tools, semi-finished bone products, and bone debris. Pottery kilns were also found north and northwest of the site. Residential areas and burials were scattered over the site (Figure 12). Medium-sized burials in several locations contained bronze, jade, and ceramic ritual objects which were absent in small tombs (Erlitou 1984, 1992; Institute of Archaeology 1999; Zhao 1987).

Jade ritual objects often constitute a part of burial goods in elite tombs. Since jade workshops have not been identified at Erlitou, and the Yiluo region lacks jade resources, it is possible that Erlitou elites obtained jade objects from other regions through long-distance exchange.

White pottery vessels, in the most recurrent forms of *he*, *gui*, and *jue*, have been found in elite burials and palatial areas at Erlitou (Figure 13: A1-3) (Institute of Archaeology 1995: 32, 34). The *gui* and *he* vessels were used for heating liquid and pouring water or alcoholic beverages, and the *jue* vessels were used as drinking goblets. Together, these vessels facilitated ritual ceremony, most likely ancestral worship, which may have involved drinking. White pottery was made of kaolin, the material used for making porcelain in later historical times. The temperature required to fire white pottery was probably up to 1200°C (Shandong Bureau 1974: 51). Kaolin resources are available in the Yiluo region, mainly distributed in Gongyi, Yiyang, and Xin'an (Yang 1991b: 44-6), and those in Gongyi may have provided the raw material for making Erlitou white pottery (see below).

During Phase II of the Erlitou culture (*c.* 1800-1700 BC) white

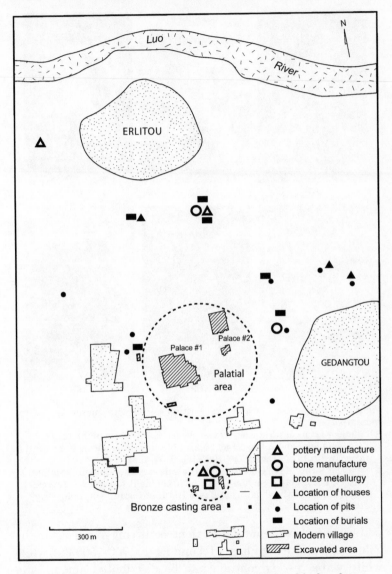

Figure 12. Map of the Erlitou site (redrawn from Institute of Archaeology 1999: fig. 7).

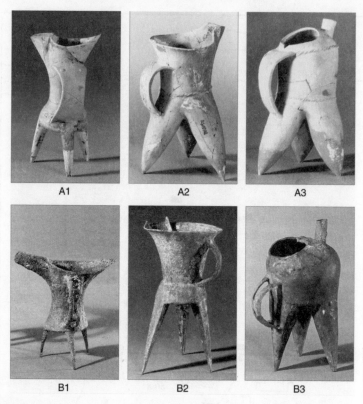

Figure 13. Comparison of white pottery ritual vessels with their bronze counterparts.
A1-3: major forms of white pottery vessels: A1: *jue* (18.6 cm high), A2 *gui* (26.1 cm high), and A3 *he* (28cm high); all from Erlitou dating to Phase II (after Institute of Archaeology 1995: figs 5, 54, 122)
B1-3: major forms of the earliest bronze vessels corresponding to the white pottery: B1: *jue* (14.8 cm high), B2: *jia* (30 cm high), and B3: *he* (24.5 cm high); all from Erlitou dating to Phase III (after Institute of Archaeology 1993: figs 92, 92-1, 93-2).

pottery vessels were most prevalent, occurring in burials in the Yiluo region. During Phases III and IV (*c.* 1700-1500 BC), while white ware vessels continued to be distributed among elite burials in the Yiluo and surrounding regions, ritual bronze vessels appeared in the high elite burials only at the Erlitou site

(Liu in press).[3] This phenomenon suggests an increase in institutionalized social stratification during the Erlitou period.

Production of bronze ritual vessels was a turning point in the evolutionary process of the Erlitou political economy. Bronze vessels became the most important symbols of political, religious and economic power throughout the Bronze Age of China (Chang 1983, 1991). The technology used for making these vessels, multi-piece mould techniques, was the most important innovation which enabled such sophisticated production (Bagley 1987; Barnard 1961, 1975; Chase 1983; Franklin 1983; Gettens 1969). Although the bronze foundries at Erlitou have been dated as early as Phase II, the first bronze vessels did not occur before Phase III. Multi-piece mould techniques may therefore have developed in Phase III.

The development of casting bronze ritual vessels may have been related to the production of ceramics, including the white pottery, which were partially made using moulds (Li 1996: 13-17). Multi-piece mould techniques, however, require higher levels of division of labour and greater control of material resources, knowledge and people than pottery production does. The earliest examples of bronze ritual vessels at Erlitou occurred in four forms: *jue, jia, he* and *ding* vessels (Institute of Archaeology 1993: 116-20) (Figure 13: B1-3), which, except for the *ding* cauldron, closely resemble the form of the above-mentioned white pottery vessels (Figure 13: A1-3). Since white pottery vessels were highly developed in Erlitou Phase II, pre-existing all corresponding types of bronze ritual vessels unearthed to date, it is likely that the forms of Erlitou bronze ritual vessels were inspired and shaped by the indigenous cultural context. The stylistic continuity of these ritual vessels over many centuries also suggests that the related ritual drinking ceremonies were similarly coeval (Liu 2003).

Bronze-casting activities were situated in high concentration and in a close proximity to the palatial area, and Erlitou bronze vessels are primarily found within the Erlitou site. This suggests that the production and distribution of ritual bronzes were clearly controlled by the high elite of the Erlitou state.

Erlitou was apparently the major centre not only for the manifestation of political and ritual power, but also for the control of a range of production. A large number of tools made of stone, bone and pottery were found at the site, including spades, axes, adzes, chisels, knives, sickles, spindle whorls, awls and needles, arrowheads, etc. (Institute of Archaeology 1999). These tools may have been used in construction for carpentry, craft production of many kinds, and agricultural activities. The population of commoners at Erlitou, therefore, seems to have included both craftsmen and peasants (Liu forthcoming).

During the Erlitou period, evidence of political centralization at the primary centre includes the following facts: a rapid increase of urban population, the construction of a palatial complex, the institutionalization of a mortuary hierarchy, the development of various craft productions, and the emergence of state-controlled craft specialization in the manufacture of ritual bronzes.

When Erlitou developed to an urban centre with a large population, which may have reached 18,000-30,000 in Phase III (Liu forthcoming), its urban population was largely engaged in architectural construction and craft production. Its subsistence economy would have required the support of agricultural producers in the hinterland of the Yiluo region.

Secondary regional centres: the control of natural resources

Erlitou sites have been found relatively densely distributed over the core area in the Yiluo basin, and form a four-tiered settlement hierarchy centred at Erlitou, indicating a centralized political and economic system. Several second-level centres, in both core and peripheral areas, have been located on major communication routes near natural resources (Figure 1).

The core: the Yiluo River valley

Several medium-sized settlements, ranging between 20 and 60 ha, have been found within an area of 25 km radius from Erlitou. Among these sites, three have been excavated and reported in reasonable detail. These are Shaochai in Gongyi, Huizui in Yanshi, and Nanzhai in Yichuan. These three sites shared one common feature: they were all located on rivers providing access to resource-rich mountainous regions nearby.

Shaochai (60 ha) is situated in Gongyi, the eastern part of the Yiluo basin, where alluvial plains meet the highlands that extend from the Songshan Mountains. An international archaeology team led by the authors has conducted regional surveys in this area since 1998, which have greatly improved our understanding of this region (Chen et al. 2003). In Gongyi the alluvial land is fertile, while the mountains are rich and diverse in resources such as stone, kaolin, iron, coal, and many types of trees (Gongxian 1989, 1991). The kaolin deposits have been used for making porcelain since the Tang dynasty (Guo and Liu 1977; Liu 1981), and may have been one of the sources for making the white ceramic vessels often unearthed from palaces and elite tombs during the Erlitou period, for the Gongyi kaolin deposits were the clay sources closest to Erlitou. However, this proposition needs to be tested with trace-element analysis and a regional settlement survey in the area of the kaolin deposits in Gongyi.

The river channels originating in the Songshan Mountains, most of which have dried up today, are short but steep. These rivers in ancient times had abundant pebbles up to a few metres thick on their riverbeds, which are still visible in many locations where they are still quarried by locals for sand and pebbles.[4]

Pebbles have been traditionally used as construction material, for paving roads and making house foundations, as can be seen in the palatial area at Erlitou.

Based on results of systematic regional surveys, a number of medium and small Erlitou sites were clustered in Shaochai, forming a three-tiered settlement hierarchy along the Wuluo River. Together with Erlitou, a four-tiered settlement hierarchy seems to have developed in the Yiluo region (Figure 1, lower left insert). This pattern indicates a state-level social organization as discussed in Chapter 2. Phytolith analysis of soil samples suggests that millet was the major staple crop in the Gongyi region, although rice has been produced in a few locations since the Neolithic period (Chen *et al.* 2003). The high agricultural potential of the land near Shaochai may have been a major factor in the development of this secondary regional centre.

Shaochai is located at the confluence of the Yiluo and Wuluo Rivers, 20 km to the east of Erlitou. The Yiluo River, a tributary of the Yellow River, was a major communication route in antiquity, along which various goods produced in the surrounding regions were transported to the major centres in the Yiluo basin. It is notable that Shaochai was not inhabited during most of the Neolithic, but suddenly developed as a regional centre during the Erlitou period, paralleling the development of the primary centre at Erlitou. The establishment of this secondary centre, therefore, may have been due to the extraction of abundant natural resources and agricultural products in the Gongyi region, as well as to its position dominating the Yiluo River, a major communication route connecting the core with other regions.

Huizui, located about 15 km southeast of Erlitou (Figure 1, lower left insert), appears to have been a regional centre for stone-tool production during the Erlitou period. It is a multi-component site, with its major occupation dating to the Erlitou period (25 ha). During the 2001 field season the Yiluo International Survey Team collected more than 400 stone artifacts from disturbed Erlitou strata, including tool blanks, flakes, grinding slabs, and semi-finished and finished tools, made from 15 types of lithic materials. Most of these artifacts are limestone (Oolitic and Dolomite) blanks, sandstone grinding slabs, and semi-finished diabase axes, adzes and chisels. All lithic materials were found in the mountainous region or in the river cobbles near the site (Chen *et al.* 2003; Ford 2001; Henan 1st Team 2003).

The predominant lithic artifacts were limestone blanks for making spades, which comprised 50% of the lithic assemblage in the survey collection (119 out of 235 identifiable tool types). Huizui seems to have particularly specialized in spade production. The finished spades may not have been entirely for local consumption, since the number of finished stone spades excavated at Huizui accounts for only 16% of the lithic assemblage from domestic features (20 out of 126) (Henan Institute 1990). It is possible that a large proportion of spades produced at Huizui was made for export to other sites (Ford 2001), although the surplus production of stone tools there may have also included other tool types.

Spades made of the two types of limestone identified at Huizui have been found at Erlitou (Institute of Archaeology 1999: 400-4), suggesting that Huizui may have supplied stone tools, especially spades, to Erlitou (Chen *et al.* 2003; Ford 2001; Henan 1st Team 2003). Given that Erlitou underwent considerable construction, which required large numbers of spades for digging, as well as many axes, adzes, and chisels for wood working, it is possible that the increasing specialization in stone tool production at Huizui was related to the growing demand for them from Erlitou during its urban expansion.

Huizui was not the only site providing tools for Erlitou, which has yielded little evidence of stone tool manufacture of its own. Since Erlitou has yielded many more lithic material types than those identified at Huizui, this urban centre may have obtained tools from a number of lithic-manufacture settlements. Several other Erlitou sites near Huizui also have yielded tool blanks during previous surveys in the region. At Xiahousi (some 5 km east of Huizui), for example, archaeologists found semi-finished stone knives (Yang 1964) and spades (collected by the Yiluo survey team in the 2002 field season).

Nanzhai is situated on a sloping terrace 0.5 km east of the Yi River, about 25 km southwest of Erlitou (Figure 1). Excavations at the site uncovered houses, kilns, ash pits, and burials (Henan Institute 1996). Among the 25 burials found, several contained white pottery vessels, indicating the relatively high social status of the occupants of the tombs. The functional activities of this settlement may have related to the resources available in the region and to nearby transportation routes. The mountainous regions to the south have copper (in Ruzhou and Lushan county) (Li 1985; Shih 1955: 99), lead (in Ruyang county) (Xia 1995: 259-60), and tin (in Ruzhou) (Shih 1955: 103). These metal deposits may have been exploited in antiquity, although we have not been able to prove it archaeologically.[5] Nanzhai was located on the major communication route, the Yi River, which connected the Yiluo region to the Han River through the Nanyang basin, as discussed above.

To summarize the data: the functions of these three regional centres in the core area were similar – to obtain and transport resources and produce specialized products for the primary centre of the early state. Settlement distribution in the Yiluo region shows a clear pattern of several subcentres closely clustered around Erlitou, a pattern which conforms to Steponaitis' model (Steponaitis 1981) for a larger tribute system channeling resources into the major centre. All of these resources – food for sustaining the urban population, timber for building houses, charcoal as fuel for casting bronzes, kaolin for making elite ceramics, lithic material for manufacturing tools, pebbles for constructing palace foundations, and metals for making bronzes – would have been in great demand by the elite at Erlitou, and the river systems in the Yiluo region facilitated the transportation of these goods. It is clear that political-economic integration between city and countryside in the core area characterizes the Erlitou state formation.

The periphery

Southern Shanxi. This region possessed abundant natural resources, especially copper deposits in the Zhongtiao Mountains and salt from the Hedong Salt Lake in Yuncheng, as discussed above. Seven Erlitou sites centred on Dongxiafeng (25 ha) have been found in the Yuncheng basin (Institute of Archaeology 1989; Zhang 1989a), and 15 sites centred on Nanguan have been discovered in the Yuanqu basin (National Museum and Shanxi Institute 1996; Tong 1998). The material culture of these two clusters of settlements have many similarities with that of the Erlitou sites located in the Yiluo basin, but they are distinct from that of the previous Longshan cultural assemblages in the region. The occurrence of the Erlitou culture in southern Shanxi therefore probably represents colonization by the Erlitou population from the core area in the Yiluo region (Liu and Chen 2000, 2001b).

The purpose of such a cultural expansion would relate to the rich natural resources available in this region. In Erlitou Phase III, Dongxiafeng (Figure 14) and Nanguan (Figure 15), judging from the finds of kilns and stone moulds for bronze casting, developed into centres of craft production, making ceramics as well as bronze weapons and tools. Both sites are situated by rivers originating in the Zhongtiao Mountains, which were rich in copper deposits. Because of the easy access to fuel available in the mountains, smelting activities probably took place in these mountainous regions. The rivers may have formed natural routes for transporting copper ingots from mining and

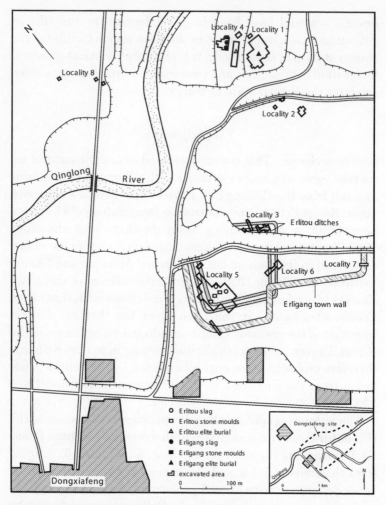

Figure 14. Map of the Dongxiafeng site, showing excavated areas and locations of artifacts relating to bronze production (redrawn from Institute of Archaeology *et al.* 1988: figs 2, 3).

smelting areas to craft centres at Dongxiafeng and Nanguan. It is important to note, however, that no evidence for casting ritual bronzes has been found at either site.

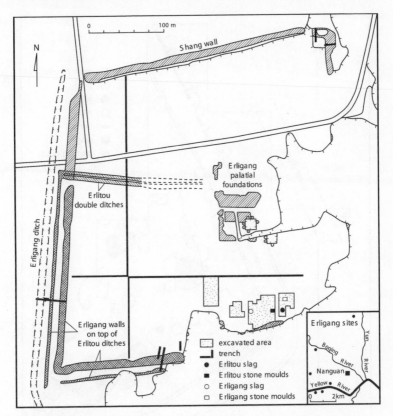

Figure 15. Map of the Yuanqu site, showing positions of the Erlitou double ditches, and locations of Erligang palatial foundations and artifacts relating to bronze metallurgy (redrawn from National Museum and Shanxi Institute 1996: fig. 3; Dong 1997: fig. 8).

At both sites craft production areas were surrounded by ditches, which were especially evident at Dongxiafeng (Figure 16). Small cave shelters, which may have been the residences of craftsmen, had been dug into the vertical walls of the ditches. Some small burials with few, if any, grave goods, probably belonging to the craftsmen, were found in the craft working area at Dongxiafeng (Institute of Archaeology *et al.* 1988). The

71

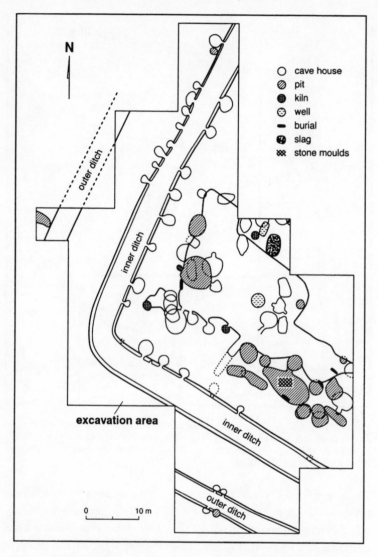

Figure 16. Craft production centre dated to Dongxiafeng Phase III (Late Erlitou), found in Locality 5 at Dongxiafeng (redrawn from Institute of Archaeology et al. 1988: fig.11).

poor living conditions, restricted residential layout, and moderate burials at these sites suggest that the social position of craftsmen was very low, and that the various forms of craft production may have been a state-controlled enterprise.

Dongxiafeng, located about 30 km to the north of the Salt Lake, was situated along the salt transportation route to the northern and eastern areas of the salt distribution region, as mentioned above. We have demonstrated elsewhere (Liu and Chen 2001b) that this regional centre played an important role as a transportation station on the northern salt route. The Nanguan site is situated at the confluence of the Boqing River and the Yellow River, and the Boqing River originated in the Zhongtiao Mountains where copper mines were abundant. Nanguan is also located immediately to the north of Dongtan, where the above-mentioned (p. 54) stone weight of the Song dynasty, used for salt transport, was discovered. Nanguan was apparently situated at a junction of the communication routes for transporting copper and salt. Today a road directly connects the Dongxiafeng area with the Yuanqu basin through the Zhongtiao Mountains (Figure 11). This route may have existed in antiquity and may have been used for salt transportation. The function of Dongxiafeng and Nanguan as regional centres, therefore, was closely related to the procurement and transport of copper and salt primarily to the core area in the Yiluo region (Liu and Chen 2001b). The functions of Dongxiafeng and Nanguan became more crystallized in the Early Shang period (see below).

Eastern Shaanxi. About eight sites with Erlitou deposits (pits and burials) have been found in the eastern part of central and southern Shaanxi, while only some isolated ceramic vessels in the Erlitou style have been identified in western Shaanxi (Zhang 1998, 2000; Zhang *et al.* 1999: 56-7). These phenomena suggest that eastern Shaanxi was the westernmost peripheral distribution of the Erlitou culture. Among these sites, Donglongshan in Shangzhou yielded the greatest concentration of material remains from this period (Wang and Yang 1997; Wang 1999a; Yang 2000b) (Figure 1).

Donglongshan (20 ha in area) is located on a terrace over-looking the Dan River to its south, with close proximity to the deposits of copper, lead and tin around Mt Hongyan to its north (Huo 1993) (Figure 1). According to historical texts, including *Jiu Tang Shu* (*Old Standard History of the Tang Dynasty*), *Xin Tang Shu* (*New Standard History of the Tang Dynasty*), and *Song Shi* (*Standard History of the Song Dynasty*), the copper deposits were exploited in ancient times long before the Tang dynasty, and were mined again during the Tang and Song dynasties for the casting of copper coins and bronze mirrors and vessels. The annual production of copper in the Tang dynasty, based on one calculation (perhaps overestimated), may have been up to 200 tons. Mining activities, however, ceased after the Ming dynasty (Huo 1993: 94), probably due to exhaustion of ore deposits. The Qinling Mountain ranges are also rich in various natural resources, such as wild animals and birds which would have provided exotic fur and feathers.

The Donglongshan site had a long occupation extending from the Longshan, through Erlitou, to Erligang periods. The Long-shan assemblage is similar to the Keshengzhuang variant distributed in central Shaanxi, and local ceramic types charac-terize the material remains dated to Phases I and II of the Erlitou period. Beginning in Erlitou Phase III, the ceramic assemblage changes to a style resembling that of the Erlitou culture in the Yiluo basin.

Several burials dating to Erlitou Phases I and II were asso-ciated with jade and stone ritual objects and waste products (Yang 2000a), suggesting that jade/stone manufacture took place at the site. The Shangzhou area has semiprecious stones, and its neighbouring county Lantian was well-known for pro-ducing Lantian jade from ancient times (Fang 1995: 157). The

Donglongshan people may have obtained the jade/stone material locally, although the provenance of these jade and stone items is currently unknown. We need to investigate whether the Donglongshan craftsmen produced jades for Erlitou. Archaeologists have found slag and bronze objects, including small weapons and tools, dating to the Erlitou and Erligang periods (Wang and Yang 1997; Wang 1999a). It is possible that Donglongshan was a bronze production centre. The appearance of the Erlitou culture in this resource-rich region seems to be consistent with settlement patterns observed in southern Shanxi (Table 2).

More importantly, Donglongshan was located at the junction of the western water route connecting the Yangzi River to the Yellow River valley, as discussed above. Material goods could be transported from the middle Yangzi valley northwestward up the Han and Dan Rivers, and then across the watershed in northern Shangzhou to reach the Luo River, directly leading to Erlitou in the Yiluo basin (Figure 17). Given the paucity of Erlitou sites found in eastern Shaanxi, it seems that Donglongshan's association with copper and other resources in the region, and its strategic location along a major communication route, could be conditions for expansion into this region from the core area of the Erlitou state.

Middle Yangzi River valley. The southernmost distribution of the Erlitou culture reached the Yangzi River region in Hubei and Jiangxi, where the richest copper mines in the country are located, as discussed above. In this region, Panlongcheng in Hubei may have been a regional centre concerned with the procurement of metal resources.

Panlongcheng is situated near Lake Panlong in Huangpi, Hubei. It has easy access to several major communication routes: the Yangzi River to the southeast, the Han River to the southwest, and a number of small rivers originating in the

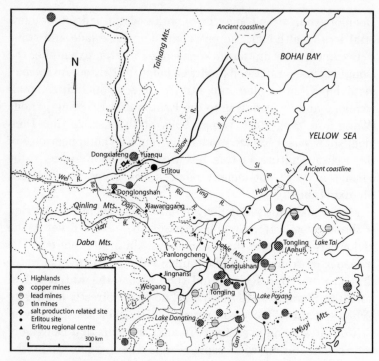

Figure 17. Locations of Erlitou settlements and metal resources on the periphery in relation to the primary centre and major regional centres in the Yellow River valley.

Dabie Mountains to the north, all of which lead directly to the Henan region (Figure 17). The location of Panlongcheng was apparently chosen for its suitability for transportation. A few hundred metres northeast of Panlongcheng, a crescent-shaped, subterranean area of magnetic abnormality, 140 m long and 20 m wide, has been found on the bank of the Panlong lake at Yangjiazui by geophysical detection. The nature of this feature is similar to that of a rammed-earth wall or a port, and the latter may be more likely, according to the report (Wang *et al.* 1998). If this inference is correct, Panlongcheng may have been used as a major transportation node (Figure 18).

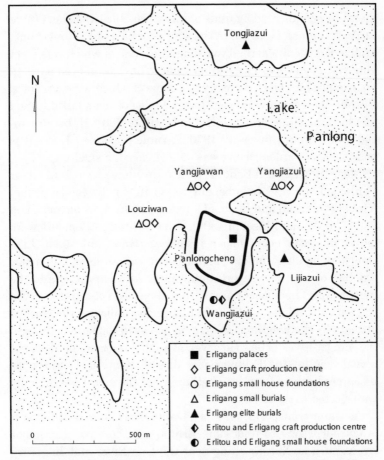

Figure 18. Plan of the Panlongcheng area, showing spatial distribution of palaces, craft production centres, residential area, and elite tombs.

Archaeologists divided the material deposits at Panlong-cheng into seven phases. Phases I-III date to a period from late Erlitou Phase II to early Lower Erligang, and Phases IV-VII date to Upper Erligang. During the Erlitou period, Panlong-cheng (c. 20 ha) was occupied by several small settlements, which may have engaged in pottery manufacture and bronze metallurgy, indicated by finds of kilns, crucibles and slag (Table 2). At Wangjiazui (3.5 ha) in the southern part of Panlongcheng, archaeologists unearthed two long kilns, one of which was 54 m long and 10 m wide. These kilns seem to have been used particularly to produce large pottery urns, some of which were crucibles. Despite the evidence for metallurgy, archaeologists failed to find moulds for casting bronzes (Hubei Institute 2001; Hubei Provincial and Beijing University 1976: 8; Wang and Chen 1987). It is possible that Panlongcheng was only engaged in smelting.

More than a dozen Erlitou culture sites have been found near Panlongcheng and in adjacent areas in northwestern Hubei (Hubei Provincial and Beijing University 1976: 8; Wang and Chen 1987: 76; Wuhan Museum 1998). Some Erlitou settlements were found in areas near copper resources (Huangshi 1984). Like Dongxiafeng and Yuanqu, Panlongcheng was situated at a major junction of water transportation routes, with easy access to the copper mines in adjacent areas (Hou 1996). The occurrence of the Erlitou cultural assemblages in this region indicates the earliest attempt by the Erlitou polity to gain access to copper resources in the Yangzi River valley. However, available information does not reveal how far the Erlitou polity directly controlled the copper resources in this region, or whether or not the metal was actually transported to the north.

As water transportation was advantageous in ancient times, it is not surprising to find some Erlitou sites located near major rivers, such as Xiawanggang near the Dan River and Jingnansi near the Yangzi River, as mentioned above. These sites may have also been the outposts of the Erlitou polity, charged with controlling the major communication routes. Erlitou material culture also reached further south into the Hunan region, as indicated by the discovery of a burial containing jade and ceramic objects, dating to the period from late Erlitou to early Erligang, at Weigang in Shimen. The site is located near the Li River, a tributary of the Yangzi River (He 1996: 62-3; Wang and Long 1987) (Figure 17).

Erlitou cultural remains, many dating to Erlitou Phase II, have also been found at sites in the northern Jiangxi region, including Guangfeng, Qianshan, Yingtan, Leping, Jiujiang, Zhangshu, Xinyu, Gaoan, and Pingxiang counties (Xu *et al.* 1994: 65). These sites are located in close proximity to copper, tin, and lead mines (Figure 17).[6] The Erlitou materials in these sites, however, occur as isolated artifacts, and the sites containing Erlitou ceramics were dominated by indigenous cultural assemblages of the region, known as the Zhuweicheng culture (Peng 1999). The northern Jiangxi and Hunan regions, therefore, were likely to have been on, or beyond, the southern frontiers of the Erlitou polity.

Interregional interactions, direct or indirect, by no means involved a one-way diffusion from north to south. Ceramic vessels and sherds impressed with geometric patterns, in the indigenous styles of the middle and lower Yangzi River valley, appeared at several major Erlitou sites in the Yellow River valley. These include Erlitou in Henan, and Dongxiafeng in Xiaxian, Ganjun in Yicheng, and Dongmaputou in Yongji, all in southern Shanxi (Peng 1987: 346-7). Stamped hardware (or protoporcelain), which was first developed in southern China (Peng 1987), has been unearthed at Erlitou (Zheng 1996: 69). The exact implications of these southern-style ceramics occurring in northern China are still unclear, since the artifacts are scarce and fragmentary. It was not until the Erligang period that the nature of interregional interactions between north and south became more developed (see below).

Erlitou state formation: social processes and dynamics

The Erlitou culture, at least throughout its central extent in Phases II-III (*c.* 1800-1600 BC), represents the first political entity that meets the criteria for a state-level society defined in

Chapter 2. The first criterion, marked social stratification, is evidenced by burial differentiation, as well as by furnished elite tombs, skeletons without grave goods buried in ash pits, and human sacrifices in the palatial complex, which were all present at Erlitou (Erlitou 1984, 1992; Institute of Archaeology 1999). The second criterion, a centralized and internally specialized government, is in evidence via the development of a palatial zone at the centre of Erlitou, containing a few dozen rammed-earth palatial foundations of several different types (Institute of Archaeology 1999: 137). The large size of the palatial zone and its central position at the site indicates a high level of political and ritual control. The different sizes and forms of palatial structures imply different control activities involved in the government administration. The third criterion, a four-tiered settlement hierarchy, is confirmed by the results of the Yiluo River survey project described above.

The production of bronze ritual vessels distinguished Erlitou from other areas in China as well as other parts of the world, as the latter regions continued to make utilitarian and ornamental objects (see Linduff 2000, 1998; Muhly 1988). Technologically, multi-piece mould methods also distinguished metallurgy at Erlitou from that in the surrounding regions, where artisans continued to use hammering and single or double stone mould techniques (Franklin 1983). The Erlitou elites seem to have monopolized the most sophisticated metallurgy technology of the time and dominated the production of bronze vessels. Since the vessels were probably used as a media for communicating with deified ancestors (Chang 1983), the Erlitou elites also controlled the most sacred ritual power, which in turn confirmed their legitimacy to rule.

In addition, the Erlitou culture was characterized by territorial expansion, which may have been driven by the need to procure key resources to support the elite and the various craft productions in the core area, as discussed above.

4. The Erlitou State: Centralization and Territorial Expansion

The distribution of an archaeological assemblage should not be taken as the equivalent to the social boundary of a political entity or an ethnic group. However, as Maceachern (1998: 114) pointed out, if 'stylistic stability, in technological processes and in the material results of those processes, exists because producers form an interacting social unit that provides a learning environment and deviation-reduction mechanisms, then it may seem permissible to assume that such groups are most often ethnic groups or subunits of such groups'. Increased degrees of standardization in ceramic types can be observed in the major centres (e.g. Erlitou and Zhengzhou) and the surrounding regions. This may correlate with an increasingly specialized mode of production, with fewer producers manufacturing a limited range of ceramics, with mass production creating greater efficiency and a high standard of uniformity and quality control. This mode of production requires a specialized, full-time labourforce with a centralized system of organization (e.g. Longacre 1999; Rice 1981, 1996). We propose that the increasing degree of standardization in craft production correlates with increasing political centralization and territorial expansion, which promoted the wide distribution of ceramic products with stylistic similarities. As craftsmen comprised an important sector of the population in the major centres, mobilization of the population by state rulers during territorial expansion would have led to the migration of craftsmen with their technology, and thus the spread of their products. In addition, the large-scale production and distribution of Erlitou and Erligang ceramic utensils may have facilitated the adoption of a new material cultural assemblage by the populations which were originally derived from different cultural groups.

Nevertheless, it is not clear to what extent the government of early states was involved in the control of ceramic production. Ceramic studies in China have focused on typology rather than production and distribution; therefore, our observations regard-

81

ing the increased standardization of pottery forms are based on
the reduction of typological variants through time, rather than
on statistic analysis. This proposition needs to be tested by
systematic studies of pottery production in the future.

The change of archaeological culture may have been affected
by many social and cultural factors in addition to political
transformation. The processes of change in material culture in
the above-mentioned areas, however, share a striking common-
ality. That is, the Erlitou materials on the periphery show little
continuity with the previous local Neolithic assemblages, but
closely resemble the Erlitou remains found in the core area in
the Yiluo basin. This phenomenon may indicate a rapid replacement of material culture on the periphery caused by population
expansion or colonization from, and cultural assimilation with,
the core area of Erlitou culture. Given the fact that all these
locations on the periphery were situated in resource-rich regions, the expansion of Erlitou culture probably involved the
material manifestation of political-economic strategies closely
relating to the procurement of copper, lead, tin, salt, and other
natural resources by the state rulers (Liu and Chen 2001b).

Recent studies of lead isotopes of 31 bronzes from the Erlitou
site suggest that the copper used for casting bronze objects
dating to Phases II and III may have derived from a single
provenance. This source was distinct from that of the bronzes
dated to the Shang dynasty, when ores were obtained from
various locations, mostly in south China. Moreover, analysis of
the alloy components of 13 Erlitou bronze objects indicates that
most bronzes from Erlitou Phases II and III contain less than
2% lead. Such a low percentage indicates that the lead was
probably a natural component of the copper ore. The lead and
copper of these Erlitou bronzes may therefore have been derived from the same provenance (Jin 2000). Although these
analyses have not pinpointed the exact provenance of the Erlitou copper and lead, based on our study of settlement patterns,

resource distribution, and evidence for bronze casting at Dongxiafeng and Nanguan in southern Shanxi, the mines in the Zhongtiao Mountains would have been the most likely alloy sources for bronze metallurgy in this earliest stage.

Regional settlement patterns of the Erlitou culture were affected by the state-controlled procurement and transportation of vital natural resources available on the periphery. All the regional centres, in both the core area and periphery, were small in size compared to the major centre, suggesting political or military domination by the primary centre. The development of regional centres, therefore, was associated with population expansion from the core area, and through those outposts Erlitou obtained various resources to support the state-controlled bronze production in the primary centre.

Core-periphery interactions were accompanied by increased integration of urban and rural areas in the Yiluo region, which enhanced the rapid urban development at Erlitou, discussed above. Such a centralized political-economic system dominating a very large region satisfies the concept of territorial state defined by Trigger (1993: 8-14). If we regard Erlitou as the first urban site, the earliest urbanism in China was not only a ceremonial and political centre as Wheatley (1971: 86-96) has emphasized, but also engaged in many economic activities, including agriculture and the craft production of both prestige and utilitarian goods.

This is not to say, however, that no independent polities coexisted with the Erlitou state. Neither is it claimed that the distribution of Erlitou cultural elements resembles the political and administrative boundary of the state in a modern sense. In the Yellow River valley, archaeological cultures other than Erlitou existed in many regions, such as the Xiaqiyuan culture in northern Henan and southern Hebei, and the Yueshi culture in Shandong. These cultures, which are distinctive, but show some influence from the Erlitou assemblages, are likely to have been politically independent of Erlitou. However, it remains unclear if, or to what extent, sites distributed within the Erlitou culture region were politically autonomous. The political influence of the Erlitou state during Erlitou Phases II and III may have covered a large region, including southern Shanxi, eastern Shaanxi, most of Henan, and northern Hubei.

According to the traditional chronology, the Xia dynasty existed in a period between 2100 and 1600 BC, which would have included a part of the late Longshan and most of Erlitou culture (Phases I-III). Based on archaeological information, however, the Longshan culture was characterized as a chiefdom-level social organization, with many small competing polities coexisting in the Yellow River valley (Liu 1996b; Underhill 1994). It was not until Phase II of Erlitou culture (c. 1800 BC) that a state-level society emerged, as demonstrated above. The rise of the early state seems to have been a relatively rapid event, with many changes in social organization taking place during a short period around Erlitou Phase II. This interpretation of Erlitou state formation does not match the traditional image of early Chinese history in which the Xia was a great dynastic power from the outset. The Xia dynasty, if it existed, may have started as a chiefdom society during its early period, and then evolved into a territorial state only during the later stages of its development.

Erligang State Centralization: The Core

Some archaeologists regard the floodplain to the east of the Taihang Mountains in today's northern Henan and southern Hebei as the area where the proto-Shang people originated. Material assemblages predating the Shang period in this region are known as Xiaqiyuan culture (Li 1989; Zou 1980). Xiaqiyuan settlements have been found along several major rivers in the area between the Taihang Mountains and the Yellow River's lower course, and two regional variants – the Huiwei variant in the south and the Zhanghe variant in the north – have been defined (Liu 1990). Some regional centres were fortified with rammed-earth enclosures, such as Mengzhuang in Huixian (Henan Institute 2000a), but none of the centres reveals a level of social complexity comparable to that at the Erlitou site. Some have argued that early Shang culture may have been derived most directly from the Zhanghe variant of the Xiaqiyuan culture (Figure 1), and that the population of the Zhanghe variant, for unknown reasons, may have moved southward to eastern Henan during the late Erlitou period (Zhang 1996, 1999b). This proposition of a proto-Shang population migration is supported by the discovery of the Lutaigang site in Qixian, eastern Henan, at which ceramic assemblages show an intrusion of the Zhanghe variant into the local Yueshi and Erlitou cultures (Zhengzhou University *et al.* 1994). As eastern Henan was a Yellow River flood area (Jing and Rapp 1995), there may be more proto-Shang sites that have been deeply buried by metres of silt deposits. A regional survey project carried out by an international team in Shangqiu has found a walled city dated to the Eastern Zhou period. This city may have been the Song city of the Spring and Autumn period (770-476 BC) built by the descendants of the Shang dynasty at the location, based on historical texts, where the proto-Shang people settled (Murowchick and Cohen 2001; Zhang and Chang 1997). It is possible that the people later referred to as the Shang were a combination of several regional populations who settled in eastern Henan during the late Erlitou period. It is also possible that these people may have then moved westward and finally replaced the Erlitou state centred in the Yiluo basin (see below).

Sociopolitical development at the Erlitou site in Phase III was followed by a decline in Phase IV. The settlement size diminished, population decreased, and Palace no. 1 was abandoned. However, Palace no. 2 was still in use, the bronze foundry continued to produce ritual vessels, the Erlitou elites were still buried with prestige goods including bronze vessels (Institute of Archaeology 1999; Liu forthcoming), and Erlitou may still have been the largest settlement in the region. The decline of Erlitou coincided with the rise of a fortified town at Yanshi, located about 6 km east of Erlitou (Henan 2nd Team 1984). Shortly after the construction of Yanshi, a new fortified settlement was established at Zhengzhou, about 75 km to the east of Yanshi (Henan Institute 2001). The material assemblages found at Yanshi and Zhengzhou, and first recognized at Erligang near Zhengzhou (Henan Cultural 1959), have been designated as part of the Erligang culture.

The Erligang culture or period is divisible into two phases: Lower and Upper Erligang. A few dozen calibrated radiocarbon dates from Yanshi, Zhengzhou, Dongxiafeng, and Yuanqu have been published (Institute of Archaeology 1991; Xia Shang Zhou

2000), and the AMS ^{14}C dates from Zhengzhou indicate that the Erligang culture covered the period 1600-1415 BC (Xia Shang Zhou 2000: 65). Given that the time frame of Erligang culture roughly coincides with the early part of Shang chronology recorded in ancient texts, and the material remains of the Erligang culture are different from those of Erlitou in terms of ceramic and architectural styles, many Chinese archaeologists have regarded Erligang sites as material remains of the early Shang period (e.g. Du *et al.* 1999; Zhao and Xu 1988).

Erligang cultural remains not only rapidly replaced Erlitou assemblages at all regional centres within the Erlitou culture distribution, but also expanded to a still broader horizon. During the Lower Erligang period, Erligang sites were distributed across an area more or less congruent with that defined by Erlitou sites, including most of Henan, southern Shanxi, eastern Shaanxi, and northern Hubei. During the Upper Erligang period, Erligang material culture expanded further to western Shandong, northern Jiangxi, northern Hunan, southern Inner Mongolia, central Shaanxi, and southern Hebei. The sites distributed around the core area in western and central Henan regions show a four-tiered settlement hierarchy (Figure 2), with Zhengzhou (2500 ha) as the primary centre and Yanshi (200 ha) as a secondary centre (Figure 19). The rank-size distribution demonstrates a very strong primate curve (Figure 3), suggesting a highly integrated political system. Compared to Erlitou culture, Erligang culture had a primary centre much greater in size – eight times as large as Erlitou, and much broader territories under the direct influence of its material culture.

Major centres

There was a shift of major centre from Erlitou to Zhengzhou during the early part of the lower Erligang period, coinciding with Erlitou Phase IV (*c.* 1600-1500 BC). During the late part of

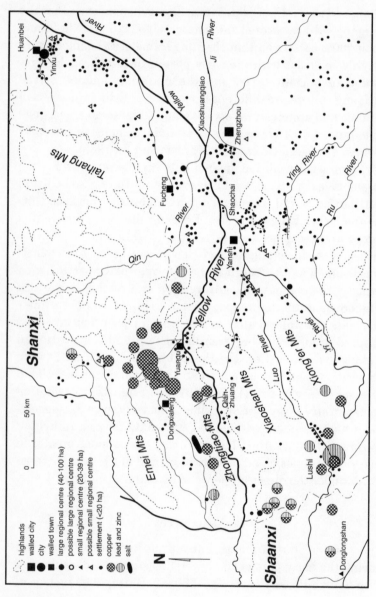

Figure 19. Distribution of sites dated to the Shang culture, settlement hierarchy, and locations of key natural resources in the Yellow River valley. Note that not all sites are contemporary.

the Lower Erligang and Upper Erligang periods, Zhengzhou quickly became the dominant centre, judging from its size and material remains. The relationship between Erlitou, Yanshi and Zhengzhou has been a matter of debate among Chinese archaeologists, mainly concerning the historical affiliations of these three sites, some of which are identified as Xia and Shang capital cities recorded in historical texts (for a summary see Gao *et al.* 1998). In the following discussion we are mainly concerned with archaeological data, which are later compared with information in traditional texts.

Yanshi

Archaeologists discovered the fortified Yanshi site in 1983. Two decades of excavations have partially revealed the progress of urban development. Material remains at Yanshi can be divided into three phases, which are comparable to Erlitou Phase IV, Lower Erligang, and Upper Erligang respectively.

During Yanshi Phase I, a group of palatial architectural structures surrounded by rammed-earth walls (4 ha) was constructed, and then a second layer comprising a rammed-earth enclosure (80 ha) was added. Chinese archaeologists refer to them as the palace town and Yanshi small city, respectively. Yanshi inhabitants also built several rows of house foundations surrounded by a rammed-earth enclosure (4 ha) on the southwestern corner inside the town walls, which may have been used as storage facilities. Bronze production was carried out in the northeastern section outside the town wall (Figure 20), although it is unclear what kind of bronze products were made there. Ceramic assemblages from the earliest occupation at the site include both Erlitou and a transitional form, which is a stylistic stage between the Xiaqiyuan and Erligang types. Many Chinese archaeologists have viewed this phenomenon as the intrusion of a new material culture into this previously Erlitou-

89

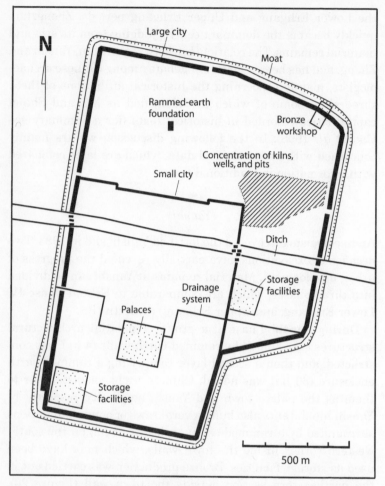

Figure 20. Plan of the Yanshi site (Redrawn from Henan 2nd team 1999: fig. 1; Wang 1999b: fig. 7).

dominant region; this transition coincides with the textually recorded conquest of the Xia by the Shang people. Some have argued that this site, now referred to as Yanshi Shangcheng (meaning the Yanshi Shang city) in archaeological literature in

China, may have functioned as the capital of the early Shang period after the conquest of Erlitou (e.g. Du *et al.* 1999: 38-40; Gao *et al.* 1998).

During Yanshi Phase II, Lower Erligang assemblages characterize the material culture. The inhabitants of Yanshi enlarged their small town into a big walled city (200 ha) with five gates. The city was an irregular rectangle in shape, with a moat surrounding the city walls. An ancient river course passed by the northeastern corner outside the city wall, an ancient lake was located to the southeast of the city, and the Luo River was about 2 km to the south of the site during early historic times. Within the city, people rebuilt and expanded the existing palaces and storage facilities several times, and constructed a second area of storage facilities outside the small city (Figure 20).

Phase III witnessed another peak of development. Yanshi inhabitants expanded the existing palaces, constructed some new palaces, and renovated storage facilities. Shortly after these developments, however, the city began to decline into an ordinary settlement before being abandoned completely in the late phase of the Upper Erligang period (*Du et al.* 1999; Gao *et al.* 1998; Wang 1999b) (Table 2).

The primary function of Yanshi in its early phase seems to have been more military than economic. It is notable that during this period Yanshi was a relatively small fortification (80 ha) coexisting with the very large Erlitou (slightly smaller then 300 ha) situated in close proximity (6 km). Erlitou, although reduced in size, was much the same as it had been during the previous periods. It functioned as an urban centre producing bronze, pottery and bone artifacts, and elite groups centred in the palatial area were active and enjoyed their privileges in mortuary practice, as discussed above. However, the Yiluo region appears to have been less peaceful. Archaeological remains at Erlitou have revealed high frequencies of arrowheads and dismembered human skeletons dating to Phase IV (Institute of Archaeology 1999: 337-41; Liu forthcoming). These suggest a period of increased conflict taking place at an inter-settlement level. But archaeological data do not tell us if the conflict occurred between the peoples of Erlitou and Yanshi, or between the people in the Yiluo region and those from outside. It is not clear, therefore, what kind of relationship existed between Erlitou and Yanshi during Yanshi Phase I, and whether or not Yanshi was the first capital of Shang dynasty.

From Phase II the population at Yanshi was apparently stratified, with palaces that may have been built exclusively for the elite, while commoners' residential areas were distributed outside of the palace zone (Henan 2nd Team 1999). As in other major centres, ceramic and bronze production were important (Figure 20). However, the bronze workshops found in the north-eastern part of the site, with no indication of vessel production, are dated only to Phase I of the Yanshi city (Henan 2nd Team 1998), when Erlitou was evidently producing bronze ritual vessels. During the Erligang period the city of Zhengzhou was established and bronze production was carried out there on a large scale (see below). It is possible that the major bronze production centre was transferred directly from Erlitou to Zhengzhou, and that Yanshi played little role in this process. Given the political and religious significance of bronze metallurgy, the change in location of bronze production from Erlitou to Zhengzhou may indicate a shift of the major political centre during the Erligang period.

Zhengzhou

Chinese archaeologists discovered the Zhengzhou walled city in the 1950s (Henan Cultural 1959). As the entire site is situated under the modern city of Zhengzhou with its population of more than a million people, excavations have been limited in scale. Our understanding of it is therefore still fragmentary.

5. Erligang State Centralization: The Core

Zhengzhou is located on the Huang-Huai floodplains. The site is surrounded by the Yellow River to the north, the hilly areas extending from the Songshan Mountains to the southwest, and the massive alluvial plains to the southeast. The northern and eastern areas of the site, which are relatively low in altitude, according to textual records, may have been covered by lakes and swamps in antiquity (An 1993: 5).

During the Erlitou period, several settlements already occupied the site. Archaeologists have uncovered abundant material remains, including pits, kilns, and burials in the northeastern part of Zhengzhou. Sections of a rammed-earth wall foundation built on top of these features and measuring 8 m wide, and more than 100 m long, date to a period immediately before the Lower Erligang (Henan Institute 1993b, 2000b). It is possible that the location may have developed into a walled centre prior to the Erligang period, but more evidence is needed to test this proposition.

Most archaeological deposits at Zhengzhou date to the Erligang period, which is further divided into four chronological phases; these are Lower Erligang Phases I and II, and Upper Erligang Phases I and II. Material remains dating to Lower Erligang Phase I are scattered; but during Lower Erligang Phase II Zhengzhou developed to a large walled city, and the entire distribution of Erligang material remains covers an area of about 2500 ha. Zhengzhou inhabitants constructed a rammed-earth enclosure as the inner city wall (300 ha), measuring 20-30 m wide at the base and 4-5 m in remaining height. They also built an outer city wall, about 12-25 m wide at the base and 5000 m in remaining length, situated 600-1100 m south and west of the inner city (Figure 21). This outer wall may have originally enclosed the entire site, since the material remains have been found within a confined area of similar radius from the inner city (Henan Institute 2001: 1-3, 177-80, 297-302; Yuan 2002).

93

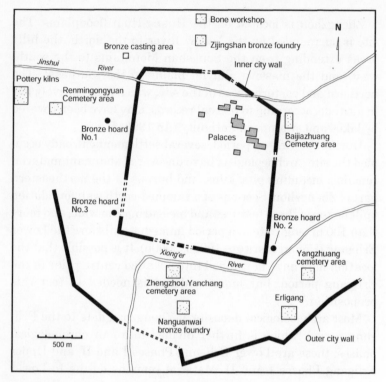

Figure 21. Plan of the Zhengzhou site (redrawn from An 1993: fig. 1; Henan Institute 1994: fig. 74).

A few dozen rammed-earth house foundations, ranging from 100 m² to 2000 m² in size, have been found inside the inner city, and were probably the remains of royal palaces and temples. Most large houses were concentrated in the northeastern part of the city, some small houses have been found in the central part, and the southern area seems to have been less populated (Henan Institute 1994: 181-8; 2001: 230-97; Pei 1993; Song 1993: 53) (Figure 21). The northeastern area near the northern wall may have been used for ritual activity, given that large erected rocks and sacrificial pits containing humans and animals

94

are located in it (Henan Institute 2001: 493-506). Some 100 human skull tops, many with saw marks, have been unearthed in a ditch near an architectural foundation. These may have been the remains of human sacrifices which took place near a temple (Hao 1993; Henan Institute 2001: 476-83). It is notable that this palatial area was situated in the same area where the pre-Erligang residential features and rammed-earth walls were found, suggesting a long period of development there.

Archaeologists found several craft production workshops for making bronze, ceramic and bone objects at the site, all located in the outer city. A bronze foundry, dating to the Lower Erligang Phase II and Upper Erligang Phase I, was located at Nanguanwai, about 700 m south of the southern inner city wall (Figure 21). Within an area of about 2.5 ha, archaeologists found copper ore, crucibles, slag, clay moulds, remains of casting processes, and smelting furnaces. Archaeologists excavated two casting areas, each surrounded by ditches. The various clay moulds and bronze artifacts from Nanguanwai foundry suggest that the major products were tools, weapons and ritual vessels. These include pickaxes, axes, adzes, *ge* dagger-axes, knives, awls, arrowheads, fishhooks, *li* vessels, *ding* caldrons, *jue* drinking vessels, *gu* goblets, *jia* vessels, basins and rings (Henan Institute 1989b; 2001: 307-67; Pei 1993).

Another bronze foundry was situated at Zijingshan, some 300 m north of the northern inner-city wall (Figure 21), and dating to the Upper Erligang Phase I. The remains of six houses, probably used as workshops, were discovered. Archaeologists also found copper ore, lead ingots, slag, clay moulds, and traces of casting. Bronze products were mainly weapons and small tools, including arrowheads, knives, chariot fittings, *yue* axes, fishhooks, hairpins, etc. A few clay moulds with elaborate designs seem to have been used for making bronze vessels. Tools made of stone, bone, and shell have been found at this bronze foundry, and some of them, such as sickles, spades, and fish-

hooks, may have been used for food production (Henan Institute
1989b; 2001: 367-84; Pei 1993).

In total 427 pieces of clay moulds have been uncovered from
Nanguanwai and Zijingshan bronze foundries. Among them
tool moulds account for 35.4%, weapon moulds 10.8%, vessel
moulds 16.6%, other moulds 4%, and unidentifiable moulds
form 33.2%. It is important to note that these two bronze
foundries were the only locations to yield hard evidence for the
casting of ritual vessels during the Erligang period. As earlier
at Erlitou, the production of bronze ritual objects was monopolized
by the highest ruling groups in the primary centre at Zhengzhou.

There may have been additional places for bronze production
at Zhengzhou. Traces of bronze casting and clay moulds were
found in an area about 500 m outside of the northwestern
corner of the inner city wall (Figure 21). But since the moulds
are too fragmentary to determine their form, it is unclear what
types of bronze objects were cast there (Zhengzhou City 1986: 28).

Mineral components of copper ores found in the bronze foundries at Zijingshan and Nanguanwai do not include lead or tin,
while the slag from the crucibles contained copper, lead, and tin.
This suggests that lead and tin were artificially mixed with
copper during the casting processes, as metal ingots may
have been brought into the primary centre from different
sources (Henan Institute 1989b; Pei 1993: 10-12). The above-
mentioned lead ingots discovered at Zijingshan seem to
support this argument.

The scale of bronze production at Zhengzhou can be inferred
based on three hoards of bronze objects discovered in the outer
city (Figure 21). A total of 28 bronzes, mostly ritual vessels –
including several large *ding* caldrons which symbolized high
political authority – were buried in abandoned wells or storage
pits. Several large square-shaped *ding* caldrons are the earliest
examples of this form. The largest *ding* caldron measures 100
cm in height and weighs 86.4 kg, and the total weight of the

entire collection exceeds 500 kg (Henan Institute 1999). These bronzes may have been cast at Zhengzhou, as the forms and decorations of some of the vessels match the moulds found at the Nanguanwai bronze foundry (Henan Institute 1999: 93-4).

Other craft workshops were found in the outer city. A ceramic production centre, 12 ha in area, was located at Minggonglu, in the western part of the outer city (Figure 21). Archaeologists discovered 14 kilns, 17 houses, 32 burials, 75 pits, and many remains of ceramic production within an excavated area of 1500 m². Most houses were small semi-subterranean structures (about 4-6 m²), which may have been potters' shelters. Ceramic production may have been highly specialized at Zhengzhou, as semi-finished products and debris near the kilns at Minggonglu appeared to be mainly in two forms, fine-paste basins and steamers (Henan Institute 1991; You 1956). A bone workshop was identified to the north of Zijingshan, from which a large number of bone materials, semi-finished bone products, bone debris, and grinding stones have been unearthed. More than 50% of these bones have been identified as human (Pei 1993: 12).

The population of Zhengzhou was clearly separated by the inner walls, with elites and their close associates primarily occupying the inner city, while commoners who were engaged in various craft productions lived within the outer city. Few domestic remains of the Erligang culture have been found in areas beyond the outer wall (An 1993: 5).

Significant numbers of tools made of stone, shell, pottery, and bone (including spindle whorls, axes, spades, awls, knives, sickles, arrowheads, and needles) have been found in both residential and craft production contexts in the outer city (e.g. Dahecun 1990; Henan Institute 1989b; 2001: 601-18, 685-709). Similar types of tools, but much fewer in quantity, have also been unearthed in the palace zone. Some of the tools may have been used for agricultural production, especially sickles and knives made of stone and shell, which have been found at many other Bronze Age sites.[1] Sickles and knives made of shells, which may have been traditionally used for harvesting grains, were frequently found in the outer city, but were nearly absent in the palace zone. For example, excavations at the Nanguanwai bronze workshop and its residential areas yielded stone and shell sickles and knives, as well as bronze fishhooks (Dahecun 1990; Henan Institute 1989b). In contrast, excavations in the palace area yielded either only a few stone implements (Henan Institute 2000b) or no tools at all (Henan Institute 1983). These phenomena suggest that the non-elite population at Zhengzhou engaged not only in craft production but also in farming, a division similar to that found at Erlitou.

Bronze products (vessels, weapon, and tools) were apparently used for ritual ceremonies, military action, craft productions such as carpentry, and the construction of palaces and city walls.[2] No bronze object can be securely categorized as an implement used in agricultural production (such as a plough or a sickle). On the other hand, agricultural tools were made of stone, bone, and shell, and in forms unchanged since the Neolithic period. As Chang (1986: 364, 410-11) has argued, early civilization was achieved in China without major change in the technology of agricultural production. This situation seems to be consistent with that of many other civilizations, such as the Inca and Aztec, in which there was no close correlation between the types of agricultural tools and either the intensity of agricultural production or the complexity of society (Trigger 1993: 33).

Zhengzhou was evidently the largest site during the Erligang period, and its development peaked in Upper Erligang Phase I. The city seems to have experienced a decline during Phase II of the same period, as all craft workshops ceased production, ditches and burials intruded into city walls, no palaces were in use, and cemeteries outside the city lack burials dating from this period (Zhang *et al.* 1993) (Table 2) The exact reasons for the decline are a matter for speculation. Based on ancient texts, which record a chaotic period due to a disordered succession in the middle-Shang period, some scholars argue that the collapse of Zhengzhou was the consequence of internal conflict among the Shang royal lineages (e.g. Chen 1987). In this case, the three bronze hoards, which are dated to a period at the very end of the Upper Erligang phase, would have been intentionally buried for safe-keeping during the political turmoil and when the capital was moved (Chen 1986: 102; Henan Institute 1999).

While Zhengzhou fell into collapse, a large settlement developed at Xiaoshuangqiao (144 ha), 20 km northwest of Zhengzhou (Figure 19), which dates to Upper Erligang Phase II (Henan Institute 1993c; Xia Shang Zhou 2000: 68-9) (Table 2). Xiaoshuangqiao was not walled, and excavations at the site found some large rammed-earth foundations, sacrificial pits, and bronze casting remains (Xia Shang Zhou 2000: 68). It is not clear, however, what kind of bronze products were made there. The function of this site has been a matter of debate among Chinese archaeologists who regard Xiaoshuangqiao either as a Shang capital named Ao (e.g. Zou 1998), or as a ceremonial locale associated with Zhengzhou (e.g. Xu and Li 1997). In any event, Upper Erligang Phase II may represent the beginning of a period of political instability.

Regional centres

Coinciding with the rise and fall of Zhengzhou, several medium-sized regional centres, some with town walls, developed in both the core and peripheral areas.

Secondary centres in the core area

Archaeologists have found large numbers of Erligang sites on the alluvial areas surrounding Yanshi and Zhengzhou, and several medium-sized sites may have been secondary or tertiary centres. Among these centres, Shaochai and Fucheng have been excavated.

Shaochai. Excavation data obtained from an area of 690 m^2 at Shaochai (Henan Institute 1993a) and regional survey data (Chen *et al.* 2003) suggest that after the Erlitou period the population at the settlement may have significantly declined during the Erligang period, and the site size was reduced to 18 ha. The fact that the major centre shifted from Erlitou to Zhengzhou means that the Yiluo region as a whole declined in political significance during the Erligang period. While Yanshi served as a secondary centre to Zhengzhou, Shaochai became a tertiary centre in the Erligang political-economic system. As in the Erlitou period, these minor centres were established to extract local resources for the primary centre. After the Erligang period, settlements in the Gongyi area nearly disappeared; this situation coincided with the abandonment of Yanshi and Zhengzhou cities (Chen *et al.* 2003).

Fucheng. This site in Jiaozuo, Henan, may have been a secondary centre near the core area. Fucheng is about 15 km south of the Taihang Mountains and 20 km north of the Qin River, which flows into the Yellow River (Figure 19). The site was occupied during a period between Erlitou Phases III and IV, and the material assemblage belongs to the Xiaqiyuan culture, believed to represent the proto-Shang culture, as mentioned above. Fucheng developed into a walled settlement (8 ha) during the Erligang period. Several palatial structures, whose foundations were found in the northeastern section of the town, were built. Both palaces and town walls were abandoned at the end of the late Upper Erligang phase (Baijiazhuang phase), as indicated by the intrusion of ash pits, dated to Upper Erligang Phase II, into the palatial foundations and town walls (Yuan and Qin 2000; Yuan *et al.* 2000). The rise and fall of this walled settlement was contemporary with comparable growth and decline of other Shang centres in central Henan and southern Shanxi, suggesting that Fucheng was a part of the Erligang political-economic system. As Fucheng was situated near the resource-rich mountainous region and water communication routes, it probably played a similar role to that of other centres – it exploited and transported resources obtained from regions immediately north of the core.

Centralization in the core

The Erligang culture can be seen as a period of rapid urbanized growth, with territorial expansion of the early state. As Zhengzhou developed into a major centre with complex urban components, Yanshi developed as a secondary centre to control resources in the Yiluo regions and the Dan River area further west. The Yi and Luo Rivers served as major communication routes for moving resources from surrounding regions through Yanshi to Zhengzhou. Large-scale storage facilities discovered at Yanshi (Wang 2000) also suggest that this urban centre functioned in this way.

The recently discovered outer city wall at Zhengzhou provides us with a new perspective on early Chinese urbanism. Urban components include not only an area for the royal lineages and craftsmen who made elite goods, but also another area for a population engaged in a wide range of occupations and specializations throughout the social spectrum. This non-elite urban population, who were protected by the outer walls, included craftsmen and peasants. The storage facilities found at Yanshi also characterize the economic functions of urban centres. As discussed in next chapter, we can achieve a better understanding of the complex functions of early cities by placing these urban centres into a broader picture of core-periphery relationships.

6

Erligang State Expansion:
The Periphery

A number of Erligang secondary regional centres have been
found on the periphery. As occurred during the Erlitou period,
these Erligang centres were much smaller in size than Zhengzhou, suggesting a high degree of political and economic control
from the major centre.

Southern Shanxi

Following the same trend of cultural change from the Erlitou to
Erligang periods in the western Henan region, the Erligang
culture replaced the Erlitou material assemblages in southern
Shanxi. The two Erlitou regional centres, Dongxiafeng in
Yuncheng and Nanguan in Yuanqu, now became fortified settlements which continued to function as bronze and ceramic production centres (Figure 19).

The rammed-earth enclosure at Dongxiafeng was about 13 ha
in area, surrounded by a moat. Procurement of copper in the
Zhongtiao Mountains may have continued, and bronze production
for making weapons and tools was carried out in the eastern part
of the site (Figure 14). An area in the southwestern corner inside
the enclosure was occupied by a group of closely spaced houses,
indicated by more than 40 circular rammed-earth foundations,
8.5-9.5 m in diameter (Figure 22) (Institute of Archaeology *et al.*
1988). These were the foundations for wooden superstructures

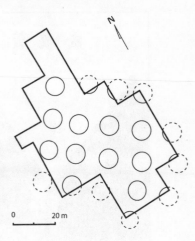

Figure 22. *Above*: Salt storage facilities at Dongxiafeng, dated to Erligang Phase; *Below*: An example of the storage structural remains, showing plan and profile of the rammed-earth foundation of this structure (redrawn from Institute of Archaeology *et al.* 1988: figs 138, 139).

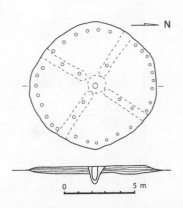

without solid earthen walls or doors, whose characteristics resemble the ancient salt storage facilities depicted in a seventeenth-century ethnohistorical compendium of Chinese technological lore, *Tiangong kaiwu* (Figure 23) (Sung 1966). Dongxiafeng may therefore have been a station on one of the ancient salt routes for transporting Hedong salt to the northern and eastern distribution regions (Liu and Chen 2000, 2001b) (Figure 11).

Figure 23. Salt storage facilities depicted in *Tiangong kaiwu (T'ien-kung k'ai-wu)*, originally printed in AD 1637 (after Sung 1966: 113).

At the same time, a walled town (13 ha) also developed at the Nanguan site in Yuanqu, referred to as Yuanqu Shangcheng (meaning the Yuanqu Shang city) by Chinese archaeologists. The southern part of the site was a centre for craft production, suggested by the discovery in this area of a stone mould for making bronze objects, metal slag, and pottery kilns. Archaeolo-

104

gists found rammed-earth foundations near the centre of the town, suggesting that palatial structures were constructed there, perhaps for administrative purposes (Figure 15). Finds also included two elite burials furnished with jade, bronze, and pottery objects, as well as a human sacrifice in the southern part of the site (National Museum and Shanxi Institute 1996). These remains suggest the existence of an elite group which was probably in charge of craft production at Yuanqu (Liu and Chen 2000, 2001b).

The function of Yuanqu as a regional centre continued, like that of Nanguan during the Erlitou period, procuring copper and transporting salt. If large-scale salt storage facilities were built at Dongxiafeng, it may have been because increased quantities of salt were being transported through the Dongxiafeng-Yuanqu route to the eastern regions (Figure 11). This implies a high demand for salt from the growing population in the primary centre at Zhengzhou.

Both Dongxiafeng and Yuanqu experienced a decline during the Upper Erligang Phase II, when these centres and small sites were abandoned. Afterwards, the Yuncheng and Yuanqu basins remained nearly depopulated until the Western Zhou in the eleventh century BC (Institute of Archaeology 1989: 40; Institute of Archaeology *et al.* 1988; Tong 1998) (Table 2).

The collapse of the settlement systems in southern Shanxi may have directly related to the procurement of resources in the region. It is possible that the thin surface layers of oxidized ores in the Zhongtiao Mountains were exhausted during the early stage of mining. As the technology of smelting sulphide ores did not develop until the Western Zhou period, the early Shang miners probably had no choice but to leave the Zhongtiao Mountains when they encountered sulphide ores in the deeper layers of copper deposits.

It is important to note that the disappearance of Shang sites in southern Shanxi during the Upper Erligang phase coincided with the expansion of Shang material culture towards the east and south, where new sources of salt and copper may have come under the control of the Erligang polity, as discussed below.

Western Henan

In Lushi county in western Henan along the upper Luo River valley, settlement patterns changed markedly in the Erligang period. While only three Erlitou sites are scattered along the Luo River (Figure 1), at least 18 sites clustered together date to the Shang period (Figure 19); later the number of Western Zhou sites drops to nine (Yang 1991b: 360-2). Lushi is situated in a mountainous region with limited arable land. However, it is one of the few areas in Henan where copper and lead occur in relative abundance. Although copper deposits are low in concentration, lead has been found in large quantities (Xia 1995: 259-60). The Shang sites are small in size, with the largest one at Quli measuring 4 ha, but all were in close proximity to copper and lead deposits. The Luo River flows eastward from the Qinling Mountains to the Yiluo Basin, connecting the resource-rich mountainous region with Yanshi. Since no major excavation has been carried out in this region, we have little knowledge about the nature of these sites. However, the sudden growth in site numbers in this metal-rich area seems to be consistent with settlement patterns in other resource-abundant mountainous regions, pointing to a similar strategy of population expansion for resource procurement during the Erligang period.

Ordos and surrounding regions

The Erligang culture also appeared in the northwestern area known as the Ordos in northern Shaanxi and southern Inner Mongolia. Archaeologists have identified Erligang material remains at Baiyan in Taigu, northern Shanxi (Jinzhong Archeo-

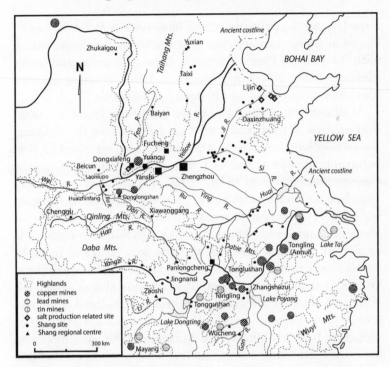

Figure 24. Locations of Erligang settlements and metal resources on the periphery in relation to primary and major regional centres in the Yellow River valley.

logy 1989), several sites in Yuxian, western Hebei (Zhangjiakou Archaeology Team 1982, 1984), and Zhukaigou in southern Inner Mongolia (Inner Mongolia 1988; Inner Mongolia and Ordos Museum 2000) (Figure 24). These sites all demonstrate distinctive regional traditions in material culture. It is especially significant that bronze ornaments such as earrings and finger rings have been found at Zhukaigou and several sites in Yuxian for the Erlitou and Erligang periods. As these ornaments rarely occurred in the Central Plains, but are commonly seen in the steppes, it is possible that non-Erlitou and non-Erligang populations may have dominated these far northwestern frontiers. During the Erligang period, however, the material assemblages at these sites are characterized by local cultures mixed with the Central Plains traditions (Inner Mongolia and Ordos Museum 2000: 285; Inner Mongolia 1990), pointing to close contacts between local and Erligang populations.

At Zhukaigou material remains have been found scattered over an area of 1 km wide and 2 km long. During the Erligang period (Zhukaigou Phase V), the site was characterized by local cultural traditions mixed with material assemblages from the Central Plains, evident in the remains of architecture, pottery vessels, clay moulds with spiral patterns (*yunleiwen*) for making pottery, and bronze weapons and ritual vessels (Inner Mongolia and Ordos Museum 2000: 278-86). A considerable proportion of relics found at the site was Erligang in style, which points to close contacts between local and Erligang populations. It is important to note that one burial was associated with a set of ceramic vessels and a bronze *ge* halberd of distinctive Upper Erligang style (Inner Mongolia 1988; Inner Mongolia Institute and Ordos Museum 2000). At Zhukaigou archaeologists found a stone mould for making axes, indicating that bronze casting was carried out there, and that the site was not far from metallic ore resources. Several bronze ritual vessels of typical Shang style were also found at the site, but there is no evidence to indicate that these vessels were produced locally. Zhukaigou may have functioned as a trade centre for communities in the northern frontiers to exchange goods with the Central Plains, as Linduff (1998: 634-43) has argued. The evidence of Erligang-style burials and the production of Erligang-style pottery at the site suggest the intrusion of an Erligang population into this remote region, and Zhukaigou may have been a regional centre that was involved in such expansion (Table 2).

Modern geological surveys located three major copper-lead mines at Bainaimiao in Siziwangqi (about 250 km northeast of Zhukaigou), and at Huogeqi and Tanyaokou in Wulatehouqi (about 300 km northwest of Zhukaigou), all in the Yin Mountains, Inner Mongolia (Zhu 1999: 195) (Figures 5, 7). The expansion of Erligang culture into these remote regions may relate to an attempt by the Erligang polity to control metal resources in the Yin Mountains. However, we need to investigate whether these metal resources were exploited during the Erligang period. Erligang influence in the Ordos seems to have been short-lived; during the late Shang period this region was dominated by regional bronze cultures with strong characteristics of the steppe culture (Linduff and Bunker 1997).

Northern Henan and southern Hebei

Many archaeologists believe that the Shang people originated here. Sites in this region of the Xiaqiyuan culture were commonly found to be contemporary with Erlitou counterparts in central and western Henan. Late Shang sites have also been found in high concentrations (Duan 1999; Heibei 1999; Liu 1990; Sino-American 1998). However, Erligang culture was underdeveloped in this region, since few sites date to this period (Wang 1998: 130). In some areas regional centres may have only begun to develop in the Upper Erligang phase, such as Taixi in Gaocheng (Heibei 1985) (Figure 24). In other areas, such as the Xingtai region, all the early Bronze Age sites date to Xiaqiyuan, and to middle and late Shang periods with no Erligang phase present (Duan 1999). Moreover, in the Huan River valley where the late Shang period primary centre was located, sites dating to the Xiaqiyuan and early Shang periods are small, and archaeologists have been unable to distinguish the Erligang phase from the Xiaqiyuan assemblages (Sino-American 1998). Given the fact that the major urban centres developed in the Zhengzhou and Yanshi areas, such cultural underdevelopment during the Erligang period in northern Henan and southern Hebei may indicate population decline in this marginal region.

The northern Henan and southern Hebei region was reoccupied by a large number of middle Shang sites (Tang 1999; Yang and Tang 1999); a newly established walled city (470 ha) at Huayuanzhuang in Anyang, known as Huanbei Shangcheng (meaning the Shang city in the north of the Huan River) (Tang *et al.* 2000), became the regional centre. This site dates to the late phase of the middle Shang period (Xia Shang Zhou 2000: 70-2),[1] which fills the gap between the Upper Erligang and Yinxu phases (Table 2). At least two medium-sized sites, Taixi in Gaocheng (larger than 10 ha) (Heibei 1985) and Caoyanzhuang in Xingtai (50 ha; Duan 1999), have yielded abundant material remains contemporary with Huanbei, and date to the middle Shang period (Figure 28).

The appearance of these middle Shang sites in northern Henan and southern Hebei points to the possibility of population migration from central Henan to the north, which followed the political instability and collapse of the settlement system centred around Zhengzhou towards the end of the Upper Erligang period.

Central and Southern Shaanxi

On the western frontiers, Erligang material assemblages replaced Erlitou occupations in the eastern part of Shaanxi and reached regions further west in central Shanxi.

Donglongshan, in the eastern part of southern Shaanxi, developed into a medium-sized site 30 ha in area when the Lower Erligang culture replaced the Erlitou assemblages. Rich archaeological remains – including burials, house foundations, pottery, bronze tools and weapons, and slag – have been discovered at the site (Wang and Yang 1997; Wang 1999a). Donglongshan may have functioned continuously as a regional centre for controlling copper resources, and as a communication node on the western route for moving material goods between south and north, as discussed above. No other Shang period sites have been found in this area, and judging from the large site size and material remains at Donglongshan, it may not have been the only settlement located along the upper Dan River valley (Figure 24) (Table 2).

Laoniupo. In eastern central Shaanxi along the Wei River valley, at least four Erligang sites have been found in an area east of Xi'an and Yaoxian. Among them Laoniupo in Xi'an may have been the regional centre (Song 1991: 71; Xi'an 1981) (Figure 24). Laoniupo is situated at the confluence of the Ba and Sha Rivers, tributaries of the Wei River. Cultural deposits at the site can be divided into six phases. Phases I and II are equivalent to the Lower and Upper Erligang, and Phases III-VI match the four phases at Yinxu (late Shang). During Phases I and II the site yielded only a few ash pits containing pottery, bone and stone tools, and oracle bones, but no bronze vessels. The material assemblages closely resemble those from the Zhengzhou area, indicating a close affiliation with the core (Song 1987, 1992; Xibei University 1988).

A copper-smelting site dating to the Erligang period was found at Huaizhenfang (5 ha) in Lantian, about 14 km southeast of Laoniupo, where large quantities of slag, charcoal, burnt clay, and remains of furnaces have been uncovered (Figure 24). Five small burials, probably belonging to the copper-smelters, were found at the site. These burials had few grave goods, some of the skeletons were dismembered, and some leg bones showed traces of amputation while the individuals were still alive. These indicate the low social status of the workers who were subjected to severe physical punishment (Xi'an 1981). The lower social status of some craftsmen at Huaizhenfang seems to be consistent with finds at the Dongxiafeng craft centre dated to the Erlitou period, as discussed above.

111

The Ba River was an ancient transport route connecting the Wei River with the Qinling Mountains, leading to southern Shaanxi. Laoniupo may have been initially set up as a communication junction by the Erligang elites to transport material goods (including copper which was smelted at Huaizhenfang) obtained from the mountains, via the Wei and Yellow Rivers, to the core region.

In contrast to Donglongshan in southern Shaanxi and the Dongxiafeng and Yuanqu site clusters in southern Shanxi, which disappeared after the Erligang phase, Laoniupo continued to exist. During the late Shang period it became a large regional centre 200 ha in area, surrounded by a cluster of small sites (Zhang *et al.* 1999: 57). Most material remains found at the site date to the late Shang period, including pottery kilns, copper-smelting and bronze-casting workshops, large-sized tombs associated with bronze ritual objects, chariot and horse sacrificial pits, houses, and large rammed-earth foundations (Song 1987; Xibei University 1988) (Table 2). Although the ritual bronzes closely resemble the style of those at Anyang, pottery types and burial customs distinct from those in the late Shang core area show increasing regional variability. A similar trend in development – material culture changing from a close affiliation with the core during the Erligang period to increasing regional variability during the late Shang period – can also be observed at another site at Beicun, Yaoxian in central Shaanxi (Archaeology Department 1994; Lei 2000) (Figure 24). This suggests a growing autonomy of some regional polities in the eastern Shaanxi area during the late Shang period.

Chenggu. Further to the southwest, archaeologists have discovered isolated Upper Erligang bronze objects in Chenggu, southern Shaanxi (Figure 24). The majority of the material remains in this region, however, are indigenous in style, and later they became more closely affiliated with the bronze culture in Sichuan during the late Shang period (Li 1983). This regional culture had some contacts with the early Shang culture in Henan, but it was not part of territories of the Shang state.

Early Bronze Age cultural occupations in these three areas in Shaanxi appear to have been different in nature. The archaeological remains of the cultural development at Donglongshan parallels those in southern Shanxi and central Henan from the Erlitou to Erligang, as all regional centres in these areas were simultaneously developed and then abandoned during the Upper Erligang period. The Laoniupo region, however, enjoyed prosperity from Erligang to late Shang periods, and reveals a tendency towards the development of regional political power. The Chenggu region received the least influence from the core area, as its indigenous culture remained dominant throughout the entire period of occupation. The development of both Donglongshan and Laoniupo was associated with the state's attempt to control copper deposits available in the Qinling Mountains. Once again this situation reveals a recurrent pattern of resource procurement and transportation, part of the processes of early state formation.

Shandong

In the east, the entire Shandong region was occupied by the Yueshi culture during the Erlitou and Lower Erligang periods. At the beginning of the Upper Erligang phase, however, more than 20 Erligang settlements appeared in western Shandong along the Ji and Si River valleys (Gao 2000; Zhang 1989b: 332-7; Zhou 1993: fig. 5). A group of Erligang settlements, centred on Daxinzhuang (30 ha) in Jinan and referred to as the Daxinzhuang variant, also appeared in northwestern Shandong. These sites were the first Erligang population intrusion into the Shandong region (Figure 24).

The Daxinzhuang variant dates to a period from the beginning of the Upper Erligang to the Yinxu phase, and its settlements gradually spread over an area that reached the Bohai Bay in the north. During the Upper Erligang period, the bronzes resembled those from Zhengzhou, while other material assemblages (including ceramics, houses, burials, etc.) consisted of two distinctive types: Type I was primarily affiliated with the Erligang culture and Type II was associated with the local Yueshi culture. The differentiation between the two sets of material remains gradually became blurred, and Type II finally disappeared during the Yinxu phase (Xu 1997, 1998a). A few Erligang sites also appeared in southwestern Shandong, along the Si River valley (Gao 2000) (Figure 24). At these sites, Erligang ceramic assemblages seem to have replaced the indigenous Yueshi material (Xu 1994). In addition, the material remains show a gradually weakened Erligang influence but increased indigenous features as one travels toward eastern Shandong (Gao 2000: 184).

It is important to note that in the Shandong region bronzes remained homogeneous in style with those from the core areas throughout the Shang period (Xu 1994: 12), while the ceramics mixed the characteristics of the Central Plains and indigenous cultures, especially in northern Shandong. Shandong possesses few small copper mines with low concentrations (Wang 1995: 198-9), and archaeologists have not found evidence of mining activities during the early Bronze Age period. This situation indicates that Erligang bronzes discovered in Shandong may have been imported from the core areas. The development of the Daxinzhuang variant and assimilation of the local Yueshi culture may reflect processes by which the early state colonized its eastern frontier, seeking coastal natural resources, including salt made from seawater.

Archaeological evidence relating to salt production in the

late Shang period has indeed been found in the coastal regions. As mentioned above, salt-making vessels, *kuixingqi*, have been found in great concentrations at four large pottery kiln sites in an area of 30 km long near Lijin (Figure 24). A large number of broken pottery vessels produced in these kilns has also been found near the sites, suggesting that salt production was carried out nearby (Wang *et al.* 1997). Given the fact that oracle-bone inscriptions recorded the presence at the Shang court of a salt official (*lu xiachen*) involved in salt production, such a large-scale and well-organized salt industry in Lijin may have been directly or indirectly controlled by the state, at least from the late Shang period in this region. It is also possible that salt production of a similar nature had already been under way during the Upper Erligang period when the state expanded into the Shandong region. Daxinzhuang was situated to the south of ancient Ji River (Tan 1982: 17-18), which connected the Bohai Bay region with the core area in Zhengzhou. As with the other regional centres, Daxinzhuang was situated in a strategic location on a communication route, along which raw materials could be transported from the eastern frontiers to the core (Figure 24; Table 2).

In southwestern Shandong, the ancient Si River was an important transport route linking the Ji and Huai Rivers, and thus connecting the Yellow River with the Lower Yangzi River region (Meng 1998) (Figure 10). Erligang expansion into this region, therefore, aimed at control of this major water transport route in order to exploit resources farther south, especially copper, lead, and tin in the Lower Yangzi River valley. This argument is supported by the discovery of several Erligang bronze vessels in Jiangsu and Anhui (see below).

In summary, the abandonment of salt production in southern Shanxi in the Upper Erligang phase related to the successful eastward expansion of the Shang state, controlling newly accessible salt and other marine resources in the coastal region (Liu and Chen 2001b). The Erligang expansion toward southwestern Shandong was associated with pursuing other key resources, such as metal, in the Lower Yangzi.

The Middle and Lower Yangzi River Valley

Following in the trajectory of the Erlitou state, the Erligang polity also expanded south, and such expansion was clearly aimed at the rich copper, tin, and lead deposits in the Yangzi River valley. The Erligang people exploited at least two major copper-mining sites in the Yangzi River valley – Tongling in Ruichang, Jiangxi (Liu and Lu 1998) and Tonglushan in Daye, Hubei (Huangshi 1999; Xia and Yin 1982) (Figure 24). Copper-mining activities at Tongling began during the Upper Erligang period. This is confirmed by the discovery of a pottery *jia* vessel of the Upper Erligang type in an underground mining area, and a ^{14}C date obtained from a wooden prop in the mineshaft (BK.89007; 3330±60) (Jiangxi Institute and Ruichang Museum 1997: 159).[2] Copper-mining activities started at the same time in the Daye region: copper-smelting sites dating to the Erligang period were found at Mianyangdi, Gutangdun, and Lihe in Daye, all located in close proximity to copper mines in the region (Huangshi 1984). Two regional centres, Panlongcheng in Hubei and Wucheng in Jiangxi, functioned as communication points established by the early state in the Central Plains to control the local resources there (Figure 24).

The Panlongcheng region. As we have seen, Panlongcheng in northern Hubei was an Erlitou craft centre. The size of the site (*c.* 20 ha) and the scale of craft production remained unchanged during the Lower Erligang period. A rapid development took place during the Upper Erligang period when the site increased in area to 100 ha. The Panlongcheng inhabitants constructed a walled town 7.5 ha in area (290 x 260 m) in the centre of the site, built palatial structures inside the town walls, and located burials, settlements, and craft production centres in the surrounding areas (Figure 18). Archaeologists discovered slag and crucibles at several locations (Hubei Institute 2001; Hubei Provincial 1976; Wang and Chen 1987), indicating that bronze metallurgy continued there. As with the Erlitou period remains at the site, no moulds have been found there, indicating that Panlongcheng may have continued to be a copper-smelting site. A total of 36 burials were uncovered, with one dating to Lower Erligang and 35 belonging to Upper Erligang. Most burials were associated with bronze ritual vessels, and four of them yielded crucibles (Hubei Institute 2001: 505-10). These burials belonged to the Panlongcheng elites, some of whom were involved in metal production. The bronze assemblages and techniques used in the construction of building foundations and town walls at Panlongcheng are similar to those used at Zhengzhou and Yanshi, and confirm its close affiliation to the north (Bagley 1999; Fang 1987; Hubei Institute 2001: 493; Hubei Provincial Museum 1976).

Judging by the lack of evidence for casting ritual vessels at Panlongcheng and the stylistic similarities between the bronzes found at Panlongcheng and major Erligang sites in the north, these ritual vessels, mainly found in elite burials, were probably cast at Zhengzhou and then imported to Panlongcheng. The same situation seems to have occurred at other regional centres, such as Dongxiafeng and Yuanqu.

Changing ceramic assemblages in the burials also reveal that Erligang cultural influence was flowing into this region. During the Lower Erligang phase, the bronzes resembled those of Zhengzhou, but the ceramics were predominantly a mixture of Erlitou style and indigenous types which previously existed in the region. Beginning in the early Upper Erligang phase when the town walls were constructed, the Erligang ceramic style gradually became dominant. By the last phase of Panlongcheng, the ceramics were overwhelmingly Central Plains in style, suggesting the full-scale cultural influence of the early state in this region (Chen 1983). This process, including the construction of the Panlongcheng town walls, the sudden expansion of the Panlongcheng site size, and the ever-increasing influence of Erligang ceramic styles, indicates that a significant Erligang population immigrated throughout that period, with the pace of immigration accelerating during the Upper Erligang period. Panlongcheng was then completely abandoned after Upper Erligang Phase II (Table 2) (Hubei Institute 2001: 447-50).

Panlongcheng town was constructed as an outpost by the Erligang state, facilitating the ultimate goal of territorial expansion into this region – the control of copper mines in the south and the transport of copper ingots to the core in the north. The existence of the town correlates with the abundant evidence for copper mining and smelting activities during the Upper Erligang period at Tongling and several sites in Daye,[3] as discussed above.

Some 150 km southwest of Panlongcheng town, ceramic assemblages consisting of Erligang and local styles have been discovered at Tonggushan and Zhangshutan in Yueyang, Hunan (Figure 24). Erligang elements, most resembling the ceramic assemblages at Panlongcheng, were the dominant cultural component at Tonggushan during the Erligang period. Material remains with an even stronger Central Plains cultural character have been found at Zhangshutan dating to the Upper Erligang Phase II (Luo 1999). As the only Erligang remains of these periods found to the east of Lake Dongting in Hunan, the two sites were likely affiliated with Panlongcheng, which is about two days' travel by river up the Yangzi from Tonggushan (Guo 1999).

Metal ingots produced in the Yangzi River region were sent north from Panlongcheng by the route through Fantang in southern Henan (the central route discussed in Chapter 3). The

She and Huan Rivers, tributaries of the Yangzi, are major water channels connecting the Panlongcheng area with the northern regions. These two rivers are close to the river systems on the northern side of the watershed in the mountains, such as the Zhugan River, which lead directly to the Huai River. More than 12 Erlitou sites and 32 Shang sites have been found in this area, mainly along the She and Huan Rivers (Song 1983). Many more sites dating to these two periods have also been found along the Huai River systems, including a large late Shang site with many elite burials at Mangzhang near the Zhugan River valley (Xinyang 1981a, 1981b). It is likely that this south-north route was one of the earliest communication channels opened during the Erlitou period, and that it was continuously used during the dynastic era.

The Gan River region. The southernmost expansion of the Erligang culture reached the Gan River valley in northern Jiangxi, where the inhabitants exploited the Tongling copper mines during the Upper Erligang period, as discussed above. The material culture in Jiangxi is characterized by the coexistence of Central Plains (the Wucheng variant) and indigenous (the Wannian variant) traditions. The Wucheng variant was mainly distributed in northern Jiangxi, while the Wannian variant was centred on northeastern Jiangxi and the surrounding regions. It is interesting to note that within the Wucheng distribution area, the two cultural traditions seem to have coexisted, with the Wucheng material being dominant in quantity, while within the Wannian distribution, Wucheng material was extremely rare. The two cultural traditions were different in many respects. They each had distinct ceramic assemblages, potters' tool kits, and inscription systems used as pottery marks. Wucheng sites frequently contained the remains of bronze metallurgy which resembles that of the Central Plains. Wannian sites, on the other hand, yield little evidence for the use of bronze, but are characterized by high-quality ceramic products. These ceramics were fired at high temperature, decorated with stamped geometric patterns, and are often referred to as stamped hardware and protoporcelain. This tradition developed locally from the stamped wares of the Neolithic period (Jiangxi Provincial and Wannian Museum 1989: 37; Li *et al.* 1990; Long *et al.* 1992; Peng 1987; Song 2000).

The material assemblages of the Wucheng variant (including ceramics, architecture, burials, and ritual activities) during the Wucheng Phase I (the Erligang period) were very similar to those of the Central Plains. Many ceramic vessels found at Wucheng variant sites are nearly identical to their counterparts discovered at Erligang sites in the north such as Zhengzhou and Dongxiafeng. Bronze tools, weapons, and ritual vessels all resembled those from the Erligang assemblages. Archaeologists have found the earliest Erligang occupations at sites concentrated in the northernmost area of Jiangxi, such as Shihuishan in De'an and Longwangling in Jiujiang. Both sites are located near the Tongling copper mines, and Shihuishan has yielded stone moulds for casting bronze tools. The recent excavation at Zhangshuzui in Ruichang unearthed a settlement in which Upper Erligang ceramic assemblages predominate. Zhangshuzui is only 2 km east of the Tongling copper mines, suggesting that its residents who originated from the north were engaged in copper mining here (Jiangxi Institute and Ruichang Museum 2000).

Erligang remains occurred slightly later in the southern region, such as Wucheng in Zhangshu (Long *et al.* 1992). These phenomena suggest a population movement from north to south (Jiangxi Institute 1997: 189; Long *et al.* 1992), a situation which corresponded to that at Panlongcheng.

In general, the Wucheng and Wannian traditions were clearly distinct from one another during the Erligang period, but began to fuse in the late Shang period. By the Western Zhou period the distinctive regional material assemblages had developed into a single culture which then became the predecessor of the Yue (Li *et al.* 1990).

Among the Wucheng variant sites, the largest one is the type-site, Wucheng in Zhangshu. The site is located to the south of the Xiao River, a tributary of the Gan River which originates from the mountainous region in the south, running northward and flowing into the Yangzi River through Lake Poyang (Figure 24). Archaeologists found Shang remains at Wucheng over a large area of 400 ha, and divided the deposits at the site into three phases which, in a general chronology, are equivalent to the Erligang, Yinxu, and Western Zhou periods. During Phase I the material remains at Wucheng are scarce, with only a few pits and isolated artifacts found. Ceramics are similar in style to those found at Zhengzhou and, as indicated by the finds of stone moulds, bronze tools were cast at the site. Although little is known about the size and layout of the site during Phase I, it seems unlikely that Wucheng was a large settlement at this time. During Phase II (late Shang period), however, Wucheng suddenly developed into a large regional centre. Archaeologists have discovered a 61 ha rammed-earth enclosure and cultural deposits up to 2 m thick over the entire area within the walled town. Excavations at the site unearthed well-constructed roads, a ritual centre with a large building and a platform made of white clay, a group of kilns for making high-quality ceramics including stamped hardware and protoporcelain, and bronze workshops for casting tools, weapons, and ritual vessels (Jiangxi Institute *et al.* 1995; Jiangxi Provincial 1987; Jiangxi Museum and Qingjiang Museum 1975, 1978; Peng 1999). In addition, archaeologists discovered a large tomb, which contained more than 480 bronze objects and is dated to the Late Shang, at Dayangzhou in Xin'gan, about 20 km east of Wucheng (Jiangxi Institute 1997). The remarkable wealth and sophisticated bronze technology found in the Dayangzhou tomb indicate the level of social complexity at Wucheng during the late Shang period. More importantly, the material culture in Wucheng Phase II developed with increasing regional characteristics distinct from those in the Central Plains (Table 2).

Metal was not the only item produced in the south which was sought after by early states in the north. Small quantities of stamped hardware and protoporcelain wares, which make up a significant percentage of the ceramic assemblages in Jiangxi, have been found at some large sites in the north. Porcelain wares from Wucheng in the south and those from Zhengzhou and Anyang in the north are similar, not only in style, but also in firing temperature (1150-1200°C for Wucheng wares and 1200±20°C for Zhengzhou wares) and in chemical composition (Li and Peng 1975; Peng 1987: 344-54). Provenance studies of these protoporcelain wares from several sites, including Wucheng, Panlongcheng, Zhengzhou, Jingnansi, and Tong-gushan, have been conducted by instrumental neutron activation analysis. The results suggest that Wucheng was a protoporcelain production centre during the Erligang period, while protoporcelain vessels found at other sites were imported (Chen *et al.* 1999), instead of being locally produced as some archaeologists have argued (An 1960). A large quantity of proto-porcelain wares and the special kilns for making such wares, known as *longyao,* the dragon kilns, were discovered at Wucheng (Jiangxi Provincial 1987), confirming that Jiangxi was the source of such products. Stamped hardware and pro-toporcelain in the north occur in extremely low frequency, are mainly found at large sites (such as Erlitou, Zhengzhou, Yuanqu, and Anyang) and are often associated with elite buri-als. The forms of these vessels in the north are also limited to a few jar types, such as *weng, zun*, and *guan*, which might be best used as transport containers. These phenomena are clearly in contrast to the situation in the south, where such wares occur in abundance and with great varieties in form, including a whole range of objects for daily use (Peng 1987: 344-53; Yang 2000a). A hardware jar containing more than 70 kg of bronze ingots dating to the Western Zhou period was unearthed at Biedun in Jiangsu (Zhenjiang City Museum 1978), suggesting that some hardware ceramics may have been used for storing and transporting metal in ancient times. It is possible that these jars were not only regarded as prestige items employed in long-distance exchange, but also functioned as containers carrying tributary goods including metal to the north.

The river systems in Jiangxi reach into surrounding regions further south and west, where more exotic materials and resources were available. Valuables such as turtle shells, pearls, and cowries were probably extracted further south, while metals – including the radiogenic lead which occurred in bronzes at Erligang, Anyang, and Dayangzhou – may have been obtained from the southwest. In this sense, Wucheng held a strategic position as a node on these important communication routes (Figure 24).

The Li River valley. Erligang material remains have been found at Zaoshi and Baota in Shimen in the Li River valley, northern Hunan (Figure 24). Zaoshi is the largest Erligang site (7 ha) discovered in Hunan to date. People at Zaoshi conducted bronze metallurgy, as indicated by the discovery of bronze tools, slag, furnaces, and stone moulds for casting bronze tools at the site (Hunan Institute 1992). Ceramic assemblages in this region reveal a stylistic combination of traditions from the Upper Erligang culture, the local region, and surrounding areas, especially Jiangxi, showing strong Erligang influence from the north (Wang 1989). After the Erligang period the Central Plains influence disappeared in the Hunan region. Ceramics became dominated by indigenous characteristics, and bronze assemblages also developed a strong regional style with some influence from the core in the north (He 1996).

The Xiangxi region in western Hunan possesses several copper deposits (Hunan Provincial Bureau 1999: 123-5), and in the late 1970s archaeologists discovered copper mines dating to the Eastern Zhou period in the Mayang mining area. Copper ores at Mayang are high in concentration, with 85% of deposits consisting of native copper. This mining area is located near the Chen River, a tributary of the Yuan River which runs from southwest to northeast and empties into Lake Dongting (Hunan Provincial Museum 1985) (Figure 24). The distance between the Mayang copper mines and the major Erligang site at Zaoshi is more than 200 km, and it is not clear whether the people at Zaoshi obtained their copper from Mayang. However, according to Shih Chang-ju's (1955) study, many ancient copper mines were distributed across the Hunan region (Figure 5). It is likely that people may have exploited some of those ancient mines located near Zaoshi during the Erligang period. The Erligang settlements, therefore, may have expanded to northwestern Hunan to control copper deposits in this region (Table 2).

It is important to note that the material culture of the Central Plains may have already arrived in the Li River region before the Upper Erligang period. This possibility is indicated by the burial containing late Erlitou/Lower Erligang material at Weigang in Shimen (He 1996), as discussed above. The Weigang burial is located across the river from Zaoshi, suggesting that the two sites were used as residential and burial areas belonging to the same settlement (Wang and Long 1987). These phenomena point to a recurrent pattern of expansion, seen in many regions, indicating movement towards the same resource-rich regions from the late Erlitou to Erligang periods. Site distribution and material remains in Hunan suggest that attempts at political expansion into the Hunan region by the early states was initiated during the Erlitou period and increased in Erligang period. It is not clear, however, if the political power of the early state in the north reached the Li River valley, as

Erligang settlements there were scarce and isolated. Such expansion suddenly halted in the late Shang period, as confirmed by the disappearance of typical Central Plains ceramic assemblages from the Li River valley (Wang 1989).

Lower Yangzi River valley. More than a dozen sites associated with Erligang material assemblages have been found along the lower Yangzi and Huai River valleys (Archaeology Department 1997; Song 1991: 177-9). Some of these sites are near the Tongling region, a copper production area in southern Anhui, where evidence for copper mining activities and sulphide-ore smelting techniques can be traced back to the early Western Zhou period. A number of Erligang bronze ritual vessels (including *jia* vessels, *jue* vessels, *gu* cups, *yan* vessels, and *ding* tripods) were also discovered in Anhui (Meng and Zhao 1985; Song 1991: 177-9; Zhang 1991) and in Lianyungang, northern Jiangsu (Li 1997a) (Figure 24). The bronzes unearthed in Anhui and Jiangsu, however, are isolated occurrences without cultural occupational deposits at these locations.

The lower Yangzi River valley had abundant forests and numerous river channels that provided fuel and facilitated transport. More than 30 ancient copper mines dating to before the Song dynasty have been found in an area of 600 km^2 (Yang 1991a; Zhang 1999a). This area was referred to as Xuzhou in 'Jiuzhou' in the pre-Qin text 'Yugong' of *Shangshu*. From Xuzhou, according to ancient texts, metals (probably including copper) were the major tribute made to the early dynastic court.

The distribution of Erligang sites and bronzes on the southeastern periphery suggests that Erligang expansion reached the lower Huai and Yangzi River valleys, where abundant natural resources were major attractions. The Erligang state expanded its power to the southeast by controlling the south-north transport route along the Si River. Based on available information, however, it is not yet clear if the Erligang actually exploited the metal deposits in the copper-rich Tongling region in Anhui.

Summary

The Middle Yangzi River region witnessed major attempts at political expansion from the core area of the Erligang state. Following in the footsteps of the Erlitou culture, the Erligang polity quickly expanded its power towards Hubei, northern Jiangxi, and northern Hunan. The objective of such expansion was to acquire the rich oxidized copper deposits in the Middle and Lower Yangzi River valley. Panlongcheng was one of the major transport nodes on the communication routes that connected the copper mines in this part of southern China with the core area of the Erligang state in the Central Plains.

While the Panlongcheng walled town was abandoned around the end of Erligang period, the Wucheng site developed into a large regional centre characterized both by clear cultural influences from the Central Plains and by increased regional components. The fall of Panlongcheng and the rise of Wucheng may have been related events, as either the Panlongcheng population moved further south to the Wucheng region or the Wucheng population destroyed the Panlongcheng settlement at the end of Erligang period. Since the major function of Panlongcheng was related to transporting resources from south to north, its collapse indicates weakened control over the copper routes by the state in the north. On the other hand, the development of a regional centre at Wucheng, with its high level of sophistication in material culture and sociopolitical complexity, points to the emergence of a polity with increased political independence from the Anyang core area during the late Shang period.

Territorial expansion and resource control in Erligang

The rapid expansion of state power in the Central Plains is confirmed by the replacement of Erlitou material by Erligang assemblages, and by the intrusions of Erligang material culture into broader regions. The changes which took place in southern Shanxi, eastern Shaanxi, western Shandong, and the middle Yangzi River valley were the result of the wholesale expansion of material culture, rather than of trade or gradual cultural diffusion. This implies population migration and colonization from the core area to the periphery. The installation of fortified towns at several previously existing Erlitou regional centres implies that the Erligang expansion was military in nature, driven by prolonged political-economic needs: to obtain and transport vital natural resources, especially copper, tin, lead, and salt.

The above discussion reveals two different processes of social change during the Upper Erligang period. The Erligang population seems to have declined in the west. Donglongshan in eastern Shaanxi was depopulated after the Erligang period. Southern Shanxi experienced the abandonment of walled towns and settlements, accompanied by the decline of large-scale salt production and transportation, copper mining, and bronze production in the Dongxiafeng and Yuanqu areas. At the same time, the Erligang culture expanded rapidly to the east and south. In the east, the establishment of a regional centre at Daxinzhuang related to an attempt to control coastal resources, including salt. In the south, the construction of the walled town and palaces at Panlongcheng, the spreading Erligang settlements in copper-rich areas, and the increase in copper mining and bronze metallurgical activities point to a great effort to control metal resources in the Middle Yangzi River valley. Such contemporary developments and declines in the peripheral regions were not

127

independent events but represent a connected shift of production centres.

The dramatic decrease in the number of Erligang settlements in southern Shanxi is related to strategic population migration organized by the state, in order to exploit newly controlled resources in the east and south. As metallurgical industries were probably state-controlled enterprises, and as some proportions of the labour forces were attached to the state, it would have been possible for the state to mobilize the population and direct migration. The occurrence of pottery vessels of the Erligang type among remains from the copper mines at Tongling in Jiangxi confirms a close affiliation between some miners and areas in the north.

As suggested above, the abandonment of the Erligang walled towns along with copper-mining activities in southern Shanxi were the result of the lack of adequate metallurgical technology needed to extract metal from sulphide ore, and of the increasing control of rich oxidized copper mines by the Erligang state in the south. The hypothesis of a shift of copper sources from the north to the south is supported by the results of lead isotopic analyses of Shang bronzes, because a considerable number of bronzes unearthed from major centres in the north were made with alloys obtained from the south. For example, the lead isotopic samples taken from several Erligang bronzes from Yanshi and Zhengzhou derived from the southern region of the distribution chart (Jin *et al.* 1998: 431). Likewise, the results of isotopic analysis on twelve bronzes from the Fuhao tomb at Yinxu of the late Shang period indicates that the metal sources were mainly from the Tonglushan area (Jin 1987).

The exhaustion of oxidized copper deposits in the Zhongtiao Mountains led to the abandonment of salt production at the Hedong salt lake. Since salt production there was highly seasonal, as discussed above, there was great demand for labour during the very short harvesting period. Copper mining and salt production were complementary industries in terms of labour management, as the Erligang population could have been directed to different production activities in different seasons. However, it would have been inefficient to maintain a large population in the walled town at Dongxiafeng for only one month of salt-harvesting each year after the mining and smelting activities ceased. In addition, salt production in southern Shanxi relied primarily on optimum weather conditions, and productivity must have been unstable, declining especially during years of high precipitation. Pollen samples collected from the Zhengzhou area confirm an episode of warm and wet conditions during Upper Erligang Phase II (Song and Jiang 2000), causing unfavourable natural conditions for salt production in the Hedong Lake at around the time when the Erligang population left southern Shanxi. Salt-making by boiling seawater on the coastal area was much less dependent on climatic conditions, and salt production there was conducted year-round. Productivity was stable and controllable by manipulating a large labour force. The shift in salt production centres was probably a decision made by the state, based on both economic efficiency and population control, a decision ultimately related to a high level of political centralization.

Items procured from the periphery by the early states were not limited to bronze alloys and salt, but may have included such valuables as protoporcelain and stamped hardware, jade, turquoise, ivory, turtle shells, cowries, and many perishable goods which have not survived in the archaeological record.

The Erligang expansion to the surrounding regions, however, was not homogeneous in nature. Two types of centre-periphery relationships can be observed. First, in the regions relatively close to the centre, the material culture was completely or primarily dominated by the Erligang style. Examples of regional centres belonging to this category include Dongxiafeng and Yuanqu in southern Shanxi, Donglongshan and Laoniupo in eastern Shaanxi, Panlongcheng in Hubei, the Wucheng area in Jiangxi, Daxinzhuang in western Shandong, and several sites in southwestern Shandong. Most of these regional centres were located at nodes of major transport routes near key resources, metal and salt. The second category of centre-periphery relationship occurred in regions further away from the core area, where Erligang material influence was considerably less dominant, occurring as isolated artifacts, individual burials, or small settlements. This situation can be seen at Zhukaigou in Inner Mongolia, Chenggu in southern Shanxi, Tongling in Anhui, and the Li River valley in Hunan. Although these regions had great potential in terms of resource procurement (e.g. the copper ores in the Yin Mountains and in Tongling, Anhui), or possessed important communication routes leading to resources in other more distant regions (e.g. Chenggu and the Li River region), the territory of Erligang state itself may have extended only to regions that were occupied by settlement systems belonging to the first category.

The Political-Economic Landscape of Early States: Modelling Centre-Periphery Relations

The first state, Erlitou, emerged from a political system in which multiple competing polities coexisted in the Central Plains. Once it had developed, it expanded rapidly toward the northwest, west, and south, strongly demonstrating the characteristics of a territorial state defined by Trigger, as discussed above. The expansion was largely motivated by the need to control and transport key resources, especially copper and salt, in order to meet the demand for the production of bronze weapons and ritual objects, and to support the growing population in the core area. The Erligang state accelerated the expansion, influenced by the same motivations. The patterns of such power/territorial expansion from the core to periphery were affected by a number of environmental and social factors.

Physiographic features

Remarkably, the distribution of settlements in the core and periphery of the Erlitou and Erligang states resembles the regional level central-place settlement system of late imperial China as discussed by Skinner (1977). Provincial capitals with greatest population densities were located in zones of high soil fertility and had easy access to water transport routes con-

131

nected with the periphery, while regional centres in the hinterland tended to be located at the nodes of transport channels. The formation of such settlement systems was greatly affected by physiographic features in China, where river basins were separated by mountain chains that provided convenient boundaries. The structure of the river systems virtually determined the location of a region's higher-level centres, and major roads linking those cities compensated for the deficiencies of the river system (Skinner 1977: 276-98). Although in the early state period societies were based primarily on a tributary economy rather than the commercial trade economy of the late imperial period, such physiographic features had already affected settlement patterns among the earliest urban formations. It is clear that the location of water transport routes and their relation to key resources was an important factor in determining the cultural and political landscapes of early states in China.

The power of ideology and status symbols

The quest for bronze alloys was a major driving force underlying territorial expansion. Bronze ritual vessels, in particular, were not only employed as the medium for the ceremonies of ancestor worship that asserted the political legitimacy of the elites, but also were used as status symbols that demonstrated social hierarchy, wealth, and power (Chang 1983). The production of prestige goods was not an innovation of the early states, since jade objects, elaborately made ceramics, and other exotic materials were used to symbolize elite authority during the Neolithic period. However, it was during the early development of the state that bronze was first used as the means of expressing the power structure, and bronze ritual objects were used to indicate social status. The symbolic power of bronzes was much greater than that of traditional prestige materials such as jade and pottery. Not only were the properties of bronze appealing –

bronze was referred to as 'beautiful metal' (*meijin*) in ancient China – but the processing of bronze ritual objects required much more complex technological and managerial skills, as well as a larger scale of manpower, than those involved in making other types of elite goods. Thus more political, economic, and religious power was associated with this new type of wealth (Liu 2003).

The tributary mode of production

From the perspective of political economy, the extent to which early states monopolized the production and distribution of bronze ritual objects may be used to measure degrees of political centralization, and thus the nature of the political structure of the states. State-controlled production and distribution of ritual vessels is revealed both by metallurgical processes and, in particular, by the locations where the ritual vessels were made. Since the products were divine in nature, the technology and production processes may also have been viewed as secret. The royal elite group with highest power therefore monopolized the right of access to the production. During the Erlitou period, the hard evidence for the production of ritual vessels – clay moulds for casting vessels – was found exclusively at the Erlitou site. Stone moulds for casting weapons and tools were found at regional centres at Dongxiafeng and Nanguan in southern Shanxi. This pattern continued during the Erligang period, since Zhengzhou is the only locale where clay moulds for casting ritual vessels have been found. At sites on the periphery where bronze casting was carried out – such as Dongxiafeng and Yuanqu in Shanxi, Wucheng and Shihuishan in Jiangxi, Zaoshi in Hunan, and Zhukaigou in Inner Mongolia – stone moulds were made for casting weapons and tools.[1] It is important to note that ritual vessels were made by piece-mould techniques using multiple inner and outer clay moulds, which required

133

high degrees of technical and managerial complexity (Bagley 1987; Barnard 1961, 1975; Chase 1983; Franklin 1983). Weapons and tools, by contrast, were made with two-piece joined stone moulds that required less technical sophistication. The technology of casting ritual vessels may have been specially controlled by a particular group of craftsmen attached to the royal court in the capital city. Considering that ritual bronzes from all regions are uniform in style during the Erlitou and Erligang periods, they may have been made at a single location in each period. These major centres therefore monopolized the redistribution of ritual vessels.

A high degree of political-economic centralization is confirmed by the large size of major centres and by the highly specialized craft productions carried out in them. Such a political-economic system is characterized, in Eric Wolf's words (Wolf 1982: 79-82), as 'the tributary mode of production', commonly seen in early territorial states. Under this form of organization, tribute is extracted from primary producers by political or military means. The deployment of labour to produce tribute is largely a function of the locus of political power. Two polar situations may be envisaged in the tributary mode of production, including 'one in which power is concentrated strongly in the hands of a ruling elite standing at the apex of the power system; and another in which power is held largely by local overlords and the rule at the apex is fragile and weak'. A ruling elite of surplus-takers standing at the apex of the power system will be strongest when it controls some strategic element in the process of production, such as hydraulic engineering, and can apply some form of coercion (Wolf 1982: 80). The social systems of the Erlitou and Erligang states to some extent closely resembled the first sub-mode of tributary production defined by Wolf. Bronze alloys and their products used for ritual and military purposes, rather than waterworks, were the most important strategic elements in the political-economic processes of the early states in China. The elite group on the highest political level had the strongest control over access to these elements. These phenomena, once again, support the hypothesis of a territorial state during the Erlitou and Erligang periods.

Centre-periphery interactions

The centre-periphery relationships in the early states in China were characterized by tributary systems through which vital raw materials and prestige goods circulated. The interactions between the core and periphery appear to have involved interdependent relationships, which may be described, in very broad terms, as a 'world system' or 'networks of interregional interaction' (cf. Stein 1999). Our analyses in the above discussions suggest that the interactions operated at the material level with political, religious, and economic ends. Regional centres on the periphery provided raw materials and exotic elite goods as tribute to the core area, to support urban growth and craft production in the major centre and to contribute to the formation of a hierarchical structure. In return, the major centre redistributed its restricted and secret craft products (mainly prestige goods including bronze ritual vessels) and exotic or scarce goods extracted from surrounding areas, such as protoporcelain and salt, to regional elites as reward.

The tributary economic system may have existed in chiefdom societies, in which 'food and goods were extracted as tribute from producers, actual distribution is characteristically to lesser figures within the chiefdom, rather than to the whole populace, and the redistributed items are often goods made by specialists, either part-time specialists locally supported by commoner production or full-time specialists supported by chiefs using some of the tribute exacted from producers' (Wright 1977: 381-2). In early states in China, the tributary economy was much larger in scale and more institutionalized than it is in chiefdoms, and tributary goods were especially focused on

135

prestige materials. However, the basic principle of such a system seems to be similar to that described by Wright. The Erlitou and Erligang tributary systems are best understood by looking at the entire process of production and distribution of bronze objects, extending from mining, smelting, and casting, to distributing the final products. Producers from the lowest level of the social system mined and smelted the metal ores, and regional centres transported ingots as tributary items to the primary centres. The highest elites in the primary centres controlled attached specialists who manufactured bronze ritual objects, and used some of the finished bronze products as gifts to reward the regional elites. These regional elites, in turn, further redistributed some of these gifts to lesser local elites, forming their regional political networks. The bronzes, however, were never distributed to the lowest level of the population. A similar pattern can be seen in the movement of exotic goods, such as the hardware ceramics and protoporcelain produced in Jiangxi. These exotic ceramics were tributary items brought from the south to the primary centres, and then redistributed from the royal elites down to regional elites near the core area. These ceramics occurred in descending frequency from primary centres to regional centres and are absent from small village sites in the north. For example, at least nine vessels (complete and fragmentary) were found at Zhengzhou before 1960 (An 1960: plate 10), while only a few sherds belonging to the same sort of vessel have been discovered at Yuanqu (National Museum and Shanxi Institute 1996: 229).

The operation of the tributary system in prestige-goods production and distribution is illustrated by the modified 'tributary model' originally demonstrated by Welch (1991: 17), as shown in Figure 25 for the Erlitou period and Figure 26 for the Erligang period. These models illustrate a close relationship between the settlement or administrative hierarchy and the political-economic structure for the production and redistribution of prestige goods during the Erlitou and Erligang periods. A four-tiered settlement hierarchy is illustrated for each case. While the raw material and exotic goods (tribute) move upward from the settlements on the lowest regional level to the primary centre, the finished prestige products (redistribution) move downward reaching the lowest regional centres but not the lowest tier of the settlement hierarchy. The exception is salt, which must have been redistributed to the entire population over an extensive region. However, salt may not have been seen or used as prestige goods. In addition, as illustrated in the models (Figures 25, 26), the early states also interacted and exchanged prestige goods with other polities beyond their frontiers, forming even larger networks of interregional interaction.

It is important to note that the production and distribution of subsistence goods in early states was less centralized than that of prestige goods. Stone tools were produced in settlements near lithic resources and distributed to consumers in both urban and rural areas (Chen *et al.* 2003; Ford 2001; Henan 1st Team 2003). Ceramic utensils were produced at the major centre as well as at each regional centre, and then distributed to the entire population, including commoners in the immediate surrounding areas. However, we know little about the exact sphere of pottery redistribution around each regional centre due to the lack of systematic ceramic analysis. It can only be generally argued that the production and distribution of ceramic utensils was carried out at regional or subregional levels. This localized ceramic production and distribution system is illustrated in Figure 27, which, in contrast to the prestige goods, shows no movement of goods between centres on the different levels of the settlement hierarchy. The stylistic similarities shared by the ceramic assemblages in different regions, therefore, was caused by use of the same technology by potters who moved with the population of the early states.

In this political-economic system, prestige goods and subsis-

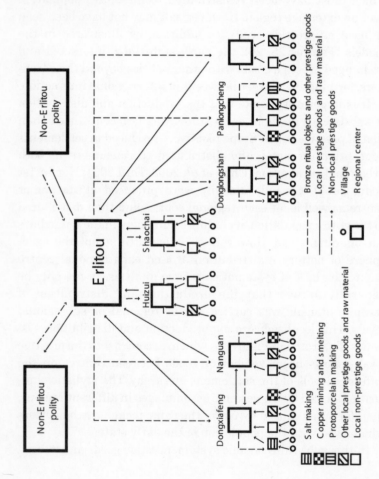

Figure 25. Tributary model of the political-economic system in the Erlitou period. Four settlement tiers form a tributary system relating to the procurement of resources and exotic goods and redistribution of prestige goods.

Non-Erlitou polity

Non-Erlitou polity

Erlitou

Panlongcheng

Donglongshan

Shaochai

Huizui

Nanguan

Dongxiafeng

Bronze ritual objects and other prestige goods

Local prestige goods and raw material

Non-local prestige goods

Village

Regional center

○ □

Salt making

Copper mining and smelting

Protoporcelain making

Other local prestige goods and raw material

Local non-prestige goods

138

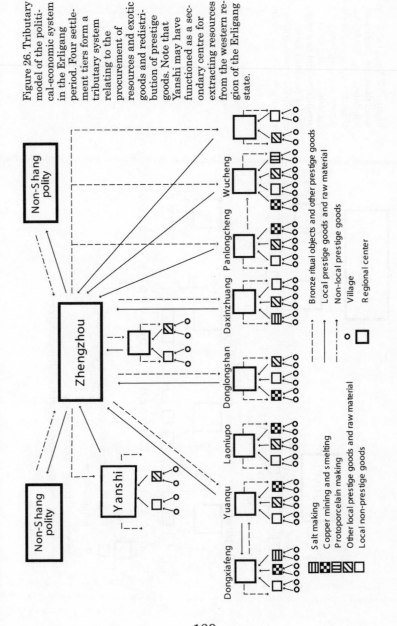

Figure 26. Tributary model of the political-economic system in the Erligang period. Four settlement tiers form a tributary system relating to the procurement of resources and exotic goods and redistribution of prestige goods. Note that Yanshi may have functioned as a secondary centre for extracting resources from the western region of the Erligang state.

139

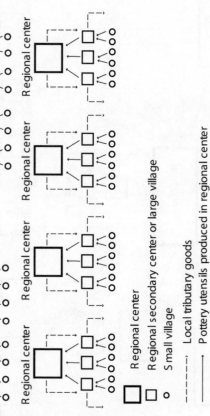

Figure 27. Model of specialized production of subsistence goods in the tributary system of early states, showing that regionally centralized production and distribution of ceramics form multiple local economic systems within the state.

tence goods were produced and circulated in different patterns, forming the economic and political backbone of the early states. This system supported the structure of political hierarchy, institutionalized the religious system especially ancestor-worship rituals (Keightley 1999), and met the basic economic demands of the entire population.

From expansion to decentralization

This highly centralized system of political economy may however have broken down towards the end of the Upper Erligang phase, when Zhengzhou and many regional centres in the core and periphery collapsed. In the meantime, other large regional centres emerged, and stylistic variations of bronze vessels accompanied by evidence for the local casting of ritual vessels occurred on a regional level.

Archaeological data provide information about the processes of cultural expansion and decline of the Erlitou and Erligang states, but not about the causal factors which may have led to such processes. Based on a cross-cultural comparative study of six pre-industrial and industrial territorial empires, Barroll (1980) reached the conclusion that imperial expansion was invoked as an alternative to the domestic redistribution of wealth. Domestic tensions associated with class stratification, redistribution, and population pressures inevitably build up in the core area of a complex society. One of the normal solutions adopted by the ruling elite was to conquer the surrounding regions in search of new sources of wealth in order to balance the redistribution among social groups in the core (Barroll 1980). As Santley and Alexander (1992) have suggested, urbanism in early states involved rapid urban expansion in the capital, creating more work in craft production, urban construction, transporting tributary goods, etc. Ultimately, the primary centre becomes much larger than would be expected, given the amount of work required, which exacerbates pressures on resources. This problem may be solved by the redistribution of population from the core to the periphery (Santley and Alexander 1992: 32-5). As a result of imperial expansion and population redistribution, new wealth may be obtained and redistributed among social groups across the spectrum of society.

This theoretical model explains the expansion of the Erlitou and Erligang states. Both states experienced a period of rapid population growth in the core coupled with territorial expansion on the periphery. New sources of wealth – metal alloys – were the underlying major stimulus directing the orientation of expansion. Some bronzes of late Shang and early Western Zhou periods bearing inscriptions of Shang royal names, and found in Hubei, Hunan and Jiangxi (Hou 1996; Liu & Lu 1997: 113), go some way to confirm that members of the Shang royal lineages were sent to the Yangzi River valley to control copper resources. A similar redistribution of population, including members of royal lineages, probably occurred in an earlier period as a strategy of wealth redistribution.

However, such expansions concealed the political crisis at the peak of development in early states: decentralization. As those newly established regional centres grew economically stronger and became integrated with local elites, they may have attempted to become more politically independent from the core. This may be the situation at the end of the Erligang period (Upper Erligang Phase II or Baijiazhuang phase). Some Chinese archaeologists refer to this period as the early part of the middle Shang period (Tang 2001), in which nearly all the Erligang centres in, and near, the core – including Zhengzhou, Yanshi, Donglongshan, Dongxiafeng, and Yuanqu – disappeared from the archaeological record, and Fucheng's town walls lost their function (Table 2). In the meantime, several large and medium centres in other regions – including Xiaoshuangqiao, Daxinzhuang, Huanbei, Caoyanzhuang, Taixi, Laoniupo, Pan-

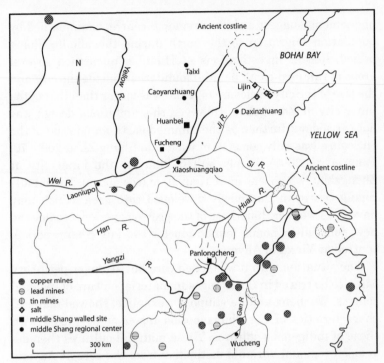

Figure 28. Distribution of major sites dating to the middle Shang period, showing decentralized political systems developed towards the end of the Erligang period; among these centres, Xiaoshuangqiao and Fucheng were abandoned in the end of Baijiazhuang phase (early phase of the middle Shang), leaving this previous core area with no large late Shang centre.

longcheng, and Wucheng – became, or continued to be, prosperous (Figure 28).

It is important to note that Xiaoshuangqiao and Fucheng were abandoned at the end of the early part of the middle Shang period, leaving this previous core area with no large late Shang regional centre. In the meantime, a large walled centre, Huanbei, as mentioned above, appeared at Huayuanzhuang in Anyang during the late part of the middle Shang period, preceding Yinxu Phase/late Shang period (Tang 2001: 41). These phenomena suggest a shift of regional centre, accompanied by population migration to the north during the middle Shang period. Recent investigations at Huanbei unearthed several areas of rammed-earth palatial foundations inside the city, and the size of the city enclosure (470 ha) was larger than that of the inner city at Zhengzhou. However, this ambitious design was not carried out further, as the rammed-earth foundation of the enclosure was only some 10 m wide (Xia Shang Zhou 2000: 70; Tang *et al.* 2000), barely half of that for the inner city at Zhengzhou, which was more than 20 m (see above). The middle Shang centre in this newly developed core area, which may have been weaker than those of the previous period, became the new political-economic foundation for the late Shang period, centred at Yinxu in Anyang.

The situation with a weakened core but stronger periphery can also be traced in the changes in material culture of regional centres. Wucheng and Laoniupo, for example, showed material characteristics of the Shang period increasingly mixed with those of indigenous cultures. These material cultures then developed regional variants distinctive from the core at Anyang during the late Shang period, while still maintaining material and ideological connections with the primary centre at Anyang. All of these changes suggest a gradual paradigm-shift from a more centralized political-economic system in the Erligang period to a more decentralized one in the late Shang period.

During the Erligang period, as the social order relied heavily on a prestige-goods economy in which the core monopolized the production and redistribution of certain types of prestige items, the social and political fabric may have been fragile. Imperial expansion and centralized core domination of peripheral centres may not have been sustainable if such networks of production and redistribution were interrupted. Such a situation accounts for the collapse of complex societies which develop a prestige-goods economy (Frankenstein and Rowlands

1978: 79), such as the complex chiefdom at Moundville in North America (Welch 1991: 194-7). In the Erligang culture, the social order would have been disturbed if the flow of metal alloys from the periphery to the core was interrupted, and if some regional centres began to make their own bronze ritual vessels as status symbols for legitimacy, in competition with those from the major centre. These were starting points for the emergence of decentralized regional hierarchical systems and autonomous polities.

As we have argued above, during the Upper Erligang phase there may have been a systematic population movement from southern Shanxi to the middle Yangzi River region directed by the early state in order to procure copper. Such an enormous undertaking may have exhausted the state administration. These events may have provoked dangerous opportunities which led to a politically unstable situation. Since archaeological data from the post-Erligang period indicate that regional centres flourished and the production of bronze ritual vessels occurred at a regional level, it is possible that the territorial state succumbed to a process of political decentralization.[2]

State formation in early China

The earliest states in China were characterized by a large urban centre in the core area which dominated the periphery where key natural resources were available. Rapid increases in the level of social complexity at the primary centre and the considerable size of state territory, both point to the existence of centralized territorial states during the Erlitou and Erligang periods. The processes of territorial expansion may have varied in time and space, but probably included military conquest, population migration, colonization, alliance formation, exchange of elite goods, and marriage.

Early states in China were characterized by the tributary

mode of political economy, focusing on a dual-system involving the production and redistribution of prestige and subsistence goods. The prestige-goods production was closely related to the belief system, which required constant supplies of metal alloys for performing the ancestor-worship ceremonies of the elite.

Finally, let us return to the four models of state formation mentioned at the beginning of this book. The size of territory and degree of political centralization in the early states resemble what Trigger described as territorial states. The city-states and segmentary states models, mainly derived from oracle-bone inscriptions of the late Shang period, may not be applicable to the Erlitou and Erligang periods. The political economy of the early states in China, however, seems different from Trigger's model for territorial states, which proposed a separated two-tier economy in which farmers manufactured necessities from locally available raw materials and exchanged these goods among themselves, while craftsmen living in cities manufactured prestige goods for elite groups. Archaeological evidence suggests that urban centres at Erlitou and Zhengzhou not only produced prestige goods such as bronzes, but also manufactured utilitarian products such as pottery and bone artifacts for the non-elite population. Pottery production at Zhengzhou was highly specialized internally, as certain kilns mainly produced certain types of vessels, suggesting a large scale of production. Furthermore, based on the tool kits discovered at Erlitou and Zhengzhou, part of the population in primary centres was also engaged in some degree of agricultural activity. This situation differs from that which Maisels depicted for the village-state model, in which the capital city had little economic function. Both Yanshi and Zhengzhou were walled in double layers, perhaps for military protection (outer wall) and as an indicator of political status (inner wall). The reasons for moving the capital varied from case to case – some cases were related to territorial control and expansion (moving from Erlitou/Yanshi to Zhengzhou), while others were caused by political conflict (the situation in the middle Shang period). The settlement system of early states in China was far more complex than that of a political/cultic centre surrounded by a large number of small villages which produced the same items by identical methods, as Maisels' analysis (Maisels 1990: 12-13, 254-61) suggests. It is obvious that none of the four models described above can be used to conceptualize state formation during the Erlitou and Erligang periods. However, with some modification, the territorial state model seems relatively close to what is observed in the archaeological data. In particular, the extensive territorial expansion of the Erlitou and Erligang states, based on archaeological evidence, resembles the political organization of a territorial state (Table 1). The concept of a segmentary state, as discussed by Keightley (2000), seems more suited to describing the political landscape of the middle and late Shang periods when the political power of the Shang core was considerably reduced while independent regional polities developed.

Furthermore, the earliest urban sites in China were indeed political and ritual centres, as Chang (1985) and Wheatley (1971) have pointed out. However, these earliest cities and towns also functioned as economic centres inhabited by a population including not only royal lineages, priests, and selected craftsmen who made elite goods, but also peasants and craftsmen who made utilitarian products. In addition, these earliest urban sites seem to have played various roles in sustaining the state within a larger political-economic system.

Our study supports Chang's argument that production of bronze ritual objects and weapons for power acquisition was one of the major components of urbanism in early China (Chang 1985). However, our research disagrees with Chang's proposition that the frequent relocations of the capital cities of the Three Dynasties were directed at chasing after new sources of metal (Chang 1986: 367). It was population expansion and the establishment of outposts or fortified towns in the periphery by the political centres in the core, rather than the moving of the capitals themselves, that were the strategies for acquisition of key resources. These strategies were practised as early as the Erlitou period, and continued until the end of the Erligang phase.

As demonstrated throughout this book, archaeological research focusing on settlement pattern and political economy has proved an effective approach for understanding the processes of state formation in early China. Archaeological data should and can be analyzed independently from traditional texts. Archaeology as a primary source of research is not simply supplementary to historical records, and we should address these two sets of information in their own terms before making connections between them.

To date there is no hard archaeological evidence to prove the historical link between the Xia dynasty and the Erlitou culture, and it is uncertain that Chinese archaeologists will find a mature writing system in the near future at Erlitou indicating that the site was a capital of the Xia dynasty. This first Chinese dynasty still remains hypothetical. Our discussion, however, illustrates a complex political and economic system centred at Erlitou, whose operation required a level of administration well beyond that of a chiefdom society. As more archaeological data becomes available in the future, we will be able to understand more fully the earliest states that developed in north China some 3800 years ago.

Notes

2. Searching for the Early State in China: Erlitou

1. Determining settlement hierarchy is an important component in settlement archaeology, providing general information about a culture's organizational complexity in terms of the number of different site types, and their size and distribution over the landscape. Levels of sociopolitical integration can be determined by studying the regional settlement system, including its range of community types (by variation in function), and the sizes and number of each type (Johnson 1977). Complex societies manifest an increased range of settlement types, as defined by function and size. A few settlements emerge as central places, while the majority are villages (Steponaitis 1981). Central places function as local administrative centres, and play various kinds of integrating roles. They differ from villages both in size (larger) and configuration (e.g. public monumental structures, fortifications, and communal granaries) (e.g. Steponaitis 1981). As complexity increases, central places may be ranked. The political capital may be a highest-order central place in other respects (e.g. economic, cultural, or ritual). Second-order central places might also function as local centres for transfer of goods and services up from lower-order centres and, reciprocally, down to the mass of population in the hinterland (e.g. Kipp and Schortman 1989). It has been argued by several anthropologists that chiefdoms may reveal up to three levels of settlement hierarchy, meaning two administrative levels (a paramount chief and local chiefs), while states are characterized by a settlement system with at least four levels of settlement hierarchy, which indicates a three-tiered administrative hierarchy above the commoners (Johnson 1973: 4-12; Wright 1984: 42). For an application of the settlement hierarchy analysis on Neolithic and Bronze Age China see Chen *et al.* 2003; Liu 1996b.

Derived from 'rank-size rule' in economic geography (Haggett 1965; Steward 1958), analysis of rank-size distribution has been used in archaeological studies of regional settlement patterns (e.g. Adams and

Jones 1981; Blanton *et al.* 1982; Johnson 1977, 1981; Kowalewski 1982; Wright 1986). Different rank-size distributions (e.g. log-normal, convex, or primate) have been seen as reflections of different systems of social integration. For instance, the rank-size distribution of highly integrated settlement systems is expected to approach log-normality. Accordingly, systems with a relatively low degree of integration should exhibit very convex rank-size distributions. Furthermore, primate distributions may have been characteristic of systems in which economic competition is minimized and/or system boundary maintenance is the primary function of the primate centre (Johnson 1981; 1987: 108-9); they also may suggest the existence of high order sacred ceremonialism, macroregional elite exchange, foreign diplomacy, and war focusing on chiefly centres (Kowalewski 1982). For an application of the rank-size analysis on the Longshan settlement patterns see Liu 1996b.

3. The Natural Landscape: Resources and Transport Routes

1. These five mines are Tongkuangyu, Xiaoxigou in Tongkuangyu, Nanhegou in Hujiayu, and Luojiahe, all in Yuanqu, and Bizigou in Wenxi (Zhu 1999: 185). In fact, the number of copper mines in the Zhongtiao Mountains is far more than these five, as many small mines have been found in Yuncheng (An and Chen 1962), Xiaxian (Xiaxian 1998), and Pinglu (Wei, Si of the Pinglu Museum 1999, personal communication). In general, the present copper mines in the Zhongtiao Mountains are low in concentration, with ores from these mines containing only 0.24-2% copper (Zhang 1995: 235-6). The Zhongtiaoshan Mineral Company, with some 20,000 employees, is engaged in copper mining and smelting in the Zhongtiao Mountains today. All shallow deposits were exhausted in antiquity, and the present-day mines are situated more than 800 m below ground level. Many copper mines are near exhaustion after years of mining (Lu, Dacheng of the Zhongtiaoshan Mineral Company 1999, personal communication).

2. In most copper deposits in the world, surface layers of copper occur as native copper and oxidized copper minerals, which have high concentrations of copper and are easy to smelt. The secondary enrichment zone below the surface layers provides sulphide ore deposits in the highest concentrations but requires more sophisticated methods for extracting the metal. The lowest zone represents the original deposit and contains copper sulphides in low concentration (Tylecote 1976: 8). The earliest evidence for smelting sulphide ore in China has been found at the Muyushan site in Tongling, southern Anhui, dating to the early Western Zhou period (*c.* eleventh century BC) (Yang 1991a). This suggests that the Erlitou and Shang people explored only oxi-

dized ore deposits because of the limited smelting techniques available at that time.

3. The major copper mines include Daye (2 million tons) in Hubei, Dexing (8.4 million tons) in Jiangxi, and Tongling (3.4 million tons) in Anhui (Zhu 1999: 185-6). Copper ores in these regions occur in high concentrations. In Tongling, for example, ores contain 10% copper on average (Liu and Lu 1997: 5).

4. The Erlitou State: Centralization and Territorial Expansion

1. The current excavation team at Erlitou has questioned the nature of this pit, based on the results of re-excavation of Palace no. 2 (Xu, Hong 2002, personal communication). The new interpretation has yet to be published.

2. These burials were found near houses. Archaeologists, however, found several burials distributed in a row on the southern bank of the Luo River, and have suggested that the Erlitou cemetery may have been located to the north of the site, as the Luo River originally flowed on the south of the site (Yue 1995). This implies that the burial area was probably destroyed by the present Luo River, which has taken its present course since the Tang dynasty, and that we may never find the high elite tombs with the most elaborate bronzes.

3. Three bronze *jia* vessels of late Erlitou style were found at Panlongcheng in Hubei (Hubei Institute 2001: fig. 299.1), and at Feixi and Liu'an in Anhui (Du 1995). However, as these items were not unearthed from excavation, there is a lack of information on their original contexts.

4. The authors observed these situations during archaeological surveys in 1998-2000.

5. Remains of bronze casting were found at Meishan in Linru (now called Ruzhou), and date to the late Longshan culture. Li Jinghua (1985) suggests that the copper ores used at Meishan may have come from the ancient mines in Ruzhou. This proposition, if proved, means that copper mines in Ruzhou were among the earliest exploited by the people in the Central Plains. It remains unclear, however, whether the Erlitou people also mined copper there.

6. These Erlitou sites are not shown on Figure 15, since the report (Xu *et al.* 1994) does not provide a map for the location of these sites.

5. Erligang State Centralization: The Core

1. For a quantitative summary of sickles and knives found at nine Shang sites, see Yang (1992: 149-55)

2. Archaeologists found tool marks on the surface of the trenches dug to form the foundation of the Shang city walls. These tool marks were caused by sharp metal implements, probably bronze pickaxes (Ma, Xiaolin 2000, personal communication).

6. Erligang State Expansion: The Periphery

1. The middle Shang period includes the late part of Upper Erligang or Baijiazhuang phase and the Huayuanzhuang phase, dating to the period *c.* 1435-1220 BC (Xia Shang Zhou 2000: 70-1).

2. It is not indicated in the publication whether or not the carbon date was calibrated. If not, the calibrated date could be even earlier.

3. The report indicated that three smelting sites in Daye belonged to the Erligang culture, but did not specify Lower or Upper Erligang period. Therefore it can only be inferred that these sites were dated to, at the latest, the Upper Erligang period.

7. The Political-Economic Landscape of Early States: Modelling Centre-Periphery Relations

1. Some Chinese archaeologists have argued for the regional production of ritual bronzes during the Shang dynasty, based on the occurrences of stone or ceramic moulds for casting bronze ritual vessels in several provinces (e.g. Xu 1998b: 231; Yang 1998), but these moulds all date to periods later than Erligang.

2. Sima Qian (*c.* 100 BC) recorded in his 'Yin benji', *Shiji* (Historical Memoirs), that from the time of king Zhongding, the Shang royal family experienced political disorder due to conflicts about succession, and as a result, regional lords stopped paying tribute to the royal court. Based on Shang royal genealogy, Zhongding ruled during the middle Shang period (Yang 1986: 207-13). This piece of the historical record thus seems to match archaeological data for the political decentralization evident in the post-Erligang period.

Bibliography

Adams, R.E.W. and Richard C. Jones (1981) Spatial Patterns and Regional Growth among Classic Maya Cities. *American Antiquity* 46: 301-22.

Adshead, Samuel Adrian M. (1992) *Salt and Civilization*. St Martin's Press, New York.

Allan, Sarah (1984) The Myth of the Xia Dynasty. *Journal of the Royal Asiatic Society of Great Britain and Ireland* 2: 242-56.

An, Jinhuai (1960) Tantan Zhengzhou Shangdai Jihe Yinwen Yingtao (On the Shang Dynasty's Hard Ceramic Wares with Stamped Geometrical Patterns Found at Zhengzhou). *Kaogu* 8: 26-8.

―――― (1993) Duiyu Zhengzhou Shangcheng 'Wai Hangtuqiang' de Kanfa (On the 'Rammed-Earth Outer Walls' of the Zhengzhou Shang City). In *Zhengzhou Shangcheng Kaogu Xin Faxian yu Yanjiu*, edited by Henan Institute of Cultural Relics, pp. 1-6. Zhongzhou Guji Press, Zhengzhou.

An, Zhimin and Cunxi Chen (1962) Shanxi Yuncheng Donggou de Dong Han Tongkuang Tiji (Eastern Han inscriptions in copper mines at Donggou in Yuncheng, Shanxi). *Kaogu* 10: 519-22.

Archaeology Department, Beijing University (1994) Shaanxi Yaoxian Beicun Yizhi 1984 Nian Fajue Baogao (Report of the 1984 Excavation Season at the Beicun Site in Yaoxian, Shaanxi). In *Kaoguxue Yanjiu*, edited by Beijing University Archaeology Department, pp. 283-342. Beijing Daxue Press, Beijing.

―――― (1997) Anhui Sheng Huoqiu, Liuan, Shouxian Kaogu Diaocha Shijue Baogao (Report of Surveys and Excavations in Suoqiu, Liuan, and Shaouxian in Abhui). In *Kaoguxue Yanjiu (3)*, edited by Beijing University Archaeology Department, pp. 240-300. Beijing Daxue Press, Beijing.

Bagley, Robert (1987) *Shang Ritual Bronzes in the Arthur M. Sackler Collections*. Harvard University Press, Cambridge, Mass.

―――― (1999) Shang Archaeology. In *The Cambridge History of Ancient China*, edited by Michael Loewe and Edward Shaughnessy, pp.124-231. Cambridge University Press, Cambridge.

Bibliography

Barnard, Neol (1961) *Bronze Casting and Bronze Alloys in Ancient China*. Australia National University and Monumenta Serica, Canberra.

―――― (ed.) (1975) *Ancient Chinese Bronzes and Southeast Asian Metal and Other Archaeological Artifacts*. National Gallery of Victoria, Melbourne.

Barnes, Gina (1993) *China, Korea and Japan: The Rise of Civilization in East Asia*. Thames and Hudson, London.

Barroll, Martin (1980) Toward a General Theory of Imperialism. *Journal of Anthropological Research* 36: 174-95.

Blanton, Richard, S. Kowalewski, G. Feinman and J. Appel (1982) *Monte Alban's Hinterland. Part 1: The Prehispanic Settlement Patterns of the Central and Southern Parts of the Valley of Oaxaca, Mexico, Memoir No. 15*. University of Michigan Museum of Anthropology, Ann Arbor.

Brook, Timothy (1989) *The Asiatic Mode of Production in China*. M.E. Sharpe, New York.

Chai, Jiguang (1991) *Yuncheng Yanchi Yanjiu*. Shanxi Renmin Press, Taiyuan.

Chang, Kwang-chih (1976) *Early Chinese Civilization: Anthropological Perspectives*. Harvard University Press, Cambridge, Mass.

―――― (1980) *Shang Civilization*. Yale University Press, New Haven.

―――― (1981) Archaeology and Chinese Historiography. *World Archaeology* 13: 156-69.

―――― (1983) *Art, Myth, and Ritual*. Harvard University Press, Cambridge, Mass.

―――― (1984) Ancient China and its Anthropological Significance. *Symbols* Spring/Fall: 2-4, 20-2.

―――― (1985) Guanyu Zhongguo Chuqi 'Chengshi' Zhige Gainian (On the Concept of Early 'City' in China). *Wenwu* 2: 61-7.

―――― (1986) *Archaeology of Ancient China*. Yale University Press, New Haven.

―――― (1991) Introduction: The Importance of Bronzes in Ancient China. In *Ancient Chinese Bronze Art: Casting the Precious Sacral Vessel*, edited by W. Thomas Chase, pp. 15-18. China House Gallery, China Institute of America, New York.

―――― (1999) China on the Eve of the Historical Period. In *The Cambridge History of Ancient China: From the Origins of Civilization to 221 BC*, edited by Michael Loewe and Edward Shaughnessy, pp. 37-73. Cambridge University Press, Cambridge.

Charlton, Thomas, and Deborah Nichols (1997) The City-State Concept: Development and Applications. In *The Archaeology of City-States: Cross-Cultural Approaches*, edited by Deborah L. Nichols and Thomas H. Charlton, pp. 1-14. Smithsonian Institution Press, Washington DC.

Bibliography

Chase, Thomas W. (1983) Bronze Casting in China: A Short Technical History. In *The Great Bronze Age of China: A Symposium*, edited by George Kuwayama, pp. 100-23. Los Angeles County Museum of Art, Los Angeles.

Chen, Gongrou (1995) Zengbo Qi Fu Ming Zhong de Jindao Xihang Ji Xiangguan Wenti (The Transport Routes of Alloys Recorded in the Inscriptions of Zheng Earl Qi's *Fu* Bronze Vessel and Related Issues). In *Zhongguo Kaoguxue Luncong*, edited by Institute of Archaeology, CASS. Kexue Press, Beijing.

Chen, Guangzu (1991) Yinxu Chutu Jinshuding Zhi Fenxi Ji Xiangguan Wenti Yanjiu (On the Metal Ingots Unearthed at Yinxu and Related Issues). In *Kaogu yu Lishi Wenhua*, edited by Wenxun Song, Yiyuan Li, Zhuoyun Xu and Kwang-chih Chang, pp. 355-88. Zhongzheng Press, Taipei.

Chen, Tiemei, George Rapp and Zhichun Jing (1999) Provenance Studies of the Earliest Chinese Protoporcelain Using Instrumental Neutron Activation Analysis. *Journal of Archaeological Science* 26: 1003-15.

Chen, Xianyi (1983) Panlongcheng Shangdai Erligang Qi Muzang Taoqi Chutan (Preliminary Study of Mortuary Ceramics at Panlongcheng During the Erligang Phase of the Shang Dynasty). In *Zhongguo Kaogu Xuehui Disici Nianhui Lunwenji*, edited by Chinese Archaeology Association, pp. 48-56. Wenwu Press, Beijing.

Chen, Xingcan, Li Liu, Yun Kuen Lee, Henry Wright and Arlene Rosen (2003) Zhongguo Wenming Fudi de Shehui Fuzahua Jincheng: Yiluohe Diqu de Juluo Xingtai Yanjiu (Development of Social Complexity in the Heartland of Chinese Civilization: Yiluo Region Settlement Patterns). *Kaogu Xuebao* 2: 161-218.

Chen, Xu (1986) Zhengzhou Duling He Huimin Shipinchang Chutu Qingtongqi de Fenxi (Analysis of Bronzes Discovered from Duling and the Huimin Food Factory at Zhengzhou). *Zhongyuan Wenwu* 4: 65-71.

—— (1987) Zhengzhou Shangdai Wangdu de Xing yu Fei (The Rise and Fall of the Shang Capital at Zhengzhou). *Zhongyuan Wenwu* 2: 112-18.

Dahecun Preservation Station, Zhengzhou city (1990) Zhengzhou Shi Mucai Gongsi Shangdai Yizhi Fajue Jianbao (Brief Report on Excavations of Shang Site at the Timber Compary in Zhengzhou City). *Huaxia Kaogu* 4: 14-29.

Denton, Derek A. (1982) *The Hunger for Salt: An Anthropological, Physiological, and Medical Analysis*. Springer-Verlag, Berlin; New York.

Dong, Qi (1997) Yuanqu Shangcheng Yizhi Shijian Niandai Yanjiu (On the Time of Initial Construction of the Yuanqu Shang City). *Zhongyuan Wenwu* 2: 39-44.

Bibliography

Du, Jinpeng (1995) Anhui Chutu Liangjian Tongjia de Niandai Jiqi Yiyi (Dates and Significance of Two Bronze *Jia* Unearthed from Anhui). In *Zhongguo Wenwubao*, 24 September, Beijing.

Du, Jinpeng, Xuerong Wang, and Liangren Zhang (1999) Shilun Yanshi Shangcheng Xiaocheng de Jige Wenti (On Several Issues Related to the Small City inside the Yanshi Shang City). *Kaogu* 2: 35-40.

Du, Zhengsheng (1991) Xiadai Kaogu Jiqi Guojia Fazhan de Tansuo (Archaeology of the Xia Dynasty and Development of the State). *Kaogu* 1: 43-56.

Duan, Hongzhen (1999) Xingxu Kaogu Jianlun (On Archaeology in the Waste of Xing). Paper presented at a Conference on Chinese Archaeology at the Turn of the Century: Retrospects and Prospects, Yixian, Hebei, 8-14 June.

Eckholm, Erik (2000) In China, Ancient History Kindles Modern Doubts. *New York Times* November 10.

Erlitou Working Team, Institute of Archaeology, CASS (1983a) 1980 Nian Qiu Henan Yanshi Erlitou Yizhi Fajue Jianbao (Brief Report of the Excavation at the Erlitou Site, Yanshi, Henan in the Fall of 1980). *Kaogu* 3: 199-205.

———— (1983b) Henan Yanshi Erlitou Erhao Gongdian Yizhi (The Palace No. 2 Remains at Erlitou, Yanshi, Henan). *Kaogu* 3: 206-16.

———— (1984) 1981 Nian Henan Yanshi Erlitou Muzang Fajue Jianbao (Brief Report on the 1981 Excavation of Burials at the Erlitou Site in Yanshi, Henan). *Kaogu* 1: 37-40.

———— (1985) 1982 Nian Qiu Yanshi Erlitou Yizhi Jiuqu Fajue Jianbao (Brief Report on the Excavation at Section Nine of the Erlitou Site in Yanshi). *Kaogu* 12: 1085-93.

———— (1992) 1987 Nian Yanshi Erlitou Yizhi Muzang Fajue Jianbao (Preliminary Report on the Excavation of Burials at the Erlitou Site in Yanshi in 1987). *Kaogu* 4: 294-303.

———— (2001) Erlitou Yizhi Tianye Gongzuo de Xinjinzhan (New Progress in the Fieldwork at the Erlitou Site). *Zhongguo Shehui Kexueyuan Gudai Wenming Yanjiu Zhongxin Tongxun* 1: 32-4.

Falkenhausen, Lothar von (1995) The Regionalist Paradigm in Chinese Archaeology. In *Nationalism, Politics, and the Practice of Archaeology*, edited by Philip L. Kohl and Clare Fawcett, pp.198-217. Cambridge University Press, Cambridge.

Fang, Weizhong (1995) *Zhongguo Ziran Ziyuan Congshu – Shaanxi Juan (Natural Resources in China – Shaanxi Juan)*. Zhongguo Huanjing Kexue Press, Beijing.

Fang, Yousheng (1987) 1987 Shilun Panlongcheng Shang Wenhua (On the Shang Culture at Panlongcheng). In *Hubei Kaogu Xuehui Lunwenji*, edited by Yousheng Fang, pp. 63-9. Wuhan Daxue Press, Wuhan.

Bibliography

Fitzgerald-Huber, Louisa (1995) Qijia and Erlitou: The Question of Contacts with Distant Cultures. *Early China* 20: 17-68.

Ford, Anne (2001) *States and Stones: Ground Stone Tool Production at Huizui, China.* Honours Thesis, La Trobe University, Melbourne.

Frankenstein, Susan and Michael Rowlands (1978) The Internal Structure and Regional Context of Early Iron Age Society in South-western Germany. *University of London Institute of Archaeology Bulletin* 15: 73-112.

Franklin, Ursula M. (1983) The Beginnings of Metallurgy in China: A Comparative Approach. In *The Great Bronze Age of China*, edited by G. Kuwayama, pp. 94-9. Los Angeles County Museum, Los Angeles.

Gao, Guangren (2000) Haidai Qu de Shangdai Wenhua Yicun (Shang Culture Remains in the Haidai Region). *Kaogu Xuebao* 2: 183-98.

Gao, Wei, Xizhang Yang, Wei Wang and Jinpeng Du (1998) Yanshi Shangcheng yu Xia Shang Wenhua Fenjie (The Yanshi Shang City and the Demarcation between the Xia and Shang Cultures). *Kaogu* 10: 66-79.

Gettens, Rutherford John (1969) *The Freer Chinese Bronzes, Volume II, Technical Studies.* Smithsonian Institution, Freer Gallery of Art, Washington, DC.

Gilley, Bruce (2000) China: Nationalism Digging into the Future. *Far East Economic Review* July 20.

Godelier, M. (1978) The Concept of the 'Asiatic Mode of Production' and Marxist Models of Social Evolution. In *Relations of Production: Marxist Approaches to Economic Anthropology*, edited by D. Seddon, pp. 207-57. Frank Cass, London.

Golas, Peter J. (1999) *Chemistry and Chemical Technology, Part XIII: Mining.* Cambridge University Press, Cambridge.

Gongxian County Chronicle Editorial Board (1989) *Gongxian Zhi.* Gongxian County Chronical Editorial Board [orig. 1929], Gongxian.

——— (1991) *Gongxian Zhi.* Zhongzhou Guji Press, Zhengzhou.

Guo, Jianbang and Jianzhou Liu (1977) Gongxian Huangye 'Tangsan-cai' Yaozhi de Shijue (Testing Excavation of the 'Tang Three-Colored Ceramics' at Huangye, Gongxian). *Henan Wenbo Tongxun* 1: 44-6.

Guo, Moruo (ed.) (1978-1982) *Jiaguwen Heji.* Zhonghua Press, Beijing.

Guo, Shengbin (1999) Shang Shiqi Dongtinghu Dong'an Qingtong Wenhua de Niandai Fenqi yu Wenhua Xingzhi (Chronology and Nature of the Shang Bronze Culture in the East of Lake Dongting). In *Kaogu Gengyun Lu*, edited by Jiejun He, pp.162-84. Yuelu Press, Changsha.

Guo, Zhengzhong (1987) Guanyu Songdai 'Yuanquxian Dianxiayang' de Jidian Kaoshi (On the 'Yuanqu County Weight' of the Song Dynasty). *Wenwu* 9: 37-40.

——— (1997) *Zhongguo Yanye Shi: Gudai Bian.* Renmin Press, Beijing.

Bibliography

Haggett, Peter (1965) *Locational Analysis in Human Geography.* Edward Arnold, London.

Hao, Benxing (1993) Shilun Zhengzhou Chutu Shangdai Rentougu Yinqi (On the Drinking Utensils Made of Human Skulls Unearthed from Zhengzhou). In *Zhengzhou Shangcheng Kaogu Xinfaxian yu Yanjiu,* edited by Henan Institute of Cultural Relics, pp. 15-20. Zhongzhou Guji Press, Zhengzhou.

He, Jiejun (1994a) Lixian Chengtoushan Xinshiqi Shidai Chengzhi (Neolithic Walled Settlement at Chengtoushan in Lixian). In *Zhongguo Kaoguxue Nianjian,* edited by Chinese Archaeology Association, pp. 239-40. Wenwu Press, Beijing.

——— (1996) Hunan Shang Shiqi Guwenhua Yanjiu (Study of the Shang Culture in Hunan). In *Hunan Sheng Bowuguan Sishi Zhounian Jinian Lunwenji,* edited by Chuanxin Xiong, pp. 47-69. Hunan Jiaoyu Press, Changsha.

He, Nu (1994b) Jingnansi Yizhi Xia Shang Shiqi Yicun Fenxi (On the Xia and Shang Remains at the Jingnansi Site). In *Kaoguxue Yanjiu (II),* edited by Beijing University Archaeology Department, pp. 78-100. Beijing Daxue Press, Beijing.

Hebei Institute of Cultural Relics (1985) *Gaocheng Taixi Shangdai Yizhi.* Wenwu Press, Beijing.

——— (1999) Hebeisheng Kaogu Gongzuo 50 Nian Huigu (Retrospects in the 50 Years of Archaeological Work in Hebei Province). *Wenwu Chunqiu* 5: 15-24.

Hemudu Archaeology Team (1980) Zhejiang Hemudu Yizhi Dierqi Fajue de Zhuyao Shouhuo (Major Gains from the Second Season of Excavation at Hemudu in Zhejiang). *Wenwu* 5: 1-15.

Henan 1st Team, Institute of Archaeology, CASS (2003) Henan Yanshi Huizui Yizhi Fajue de Xin Shouhuo (New Gains from the Excavation at Huizui Site in Yanshi, Henan), *Zhongguo Shehui Kexueyuan Gudai Wenming Yanjiu Zhongxin Tongxun* 5: 36-9.

Henan 2nd Team, Institute of Archaeology, CASS (1984) 1983 Nian Qiu Henan Yanshi Shangcheng Fajue Jianbao (Brief Report on the Excavation of the Shang City at Yanshi in Henan, 1983). *Kaogu* 10: 872-9.

——— (1998) Henan Yanshi Shangcheng Dongbeiyu Fajue Jianbao (Brief Report on Excavations on the Northeastern Part of the Yanshi Shang City, Henan). *Kaogu* 6: 1-8.

——— (1999) Henan Yanshi Shangcheng IV Qu 1996 Nian Fajue Jianbao (Brief Report of the 1996 Excavation in Section IV at the Yangshi Shang City, Henan). *Kaogu* 2: 12-23.

Henan Cultural Bureau (1959) *Zhengzhou Erligang.* Kexue Press, Beijing.

Henan Institute of Cultural Relics (1983) Zhengzhou Shangdai Chengnei Gongdian Yizhiqu Diyici Fajue Baogao. *Wenwu* 4: 1-14.

Bibliography

———— (1989a) *Xichuan Xiawanggang*. Wenwu Press, Beijing.

———— (1989b) Zhengzhou Shangdai Erligangqi Zhutong Yizhi (Bronze Casting Areas of the Erligang Phase at the Zhengzhou Shang City). *Kaoguxue Jikan* 6: 100-22.

———— (1990) Henan Yanshi Huizui Yizhi Fajue Baogao (Excavation Report of the Huizui Site in Yangshi, Henan). *Huaxia Kaogu* 1: 1-33.

———— (1991) Zhengzhou Shi Shangdai Zhitao Yizhi Fajue Jianbao (Brief Report of Excavations at the Shang Dynasty Ceramic Workshop, Zhengzhou). *Huaxia Kaogu* 4: 1-19.

———— (1993a) Henan Gongxian Shaochai Yizhi Fajue Baogao (Excavation Report on the Shaochai Site in Gongxian, Henan). *Huaxia Kaogu* 2: 1-45.

———— (1993b) Zhengzhou Huangweihui Qingniangongyu Kaogu Fajue Baogao (Report on Archaeological Excavations at Qingniangongyu in Huangweihui, Zhengzhou). In *Zhengzhou Shangcheng Kaogu Xinfaxian yu Yanjiu*, edited by Henan Institute of Cultural Relics, pp. 185-227. Zhongzhou Guji Press, Zhengzhou.

———— (1993c) Zhengzhou Xiaoshuangqiao Yizhi de Diaocha yu Shijue (Survey and Excavation at the Xiaoshuangqiao Site in Zhengzhou). In *Zhengzhou Shangcheng Kaogu Xinfaxian yu Yanjiu*, edited by Henan Institute of Cultural Relics, pp. 242-71. Zhongzhou Guji Press, Zhengzhou.

———— (1994) *Henan Kaogu Sishi Nian*. Henan Renmin Press, Zhengzhou.

———— (1996) Henan Yichuanxian Nanzhai Erlitou Wenhua Muzang Fajue Jianbao (Preliminary Report of Excavation of Erlitou Culture Burials at Nanzhai in Yichuan, Henan). *Kaogu* 12: 36-43.

———— (1999) *Zhengzhou Shangdai Tongqi Jiaocang*. Kexue Press, Beijing.

———— (2000a) Henan Huixian Shi Mengzhuang Longshan Wenhua Yizhi Fajue Jianbao (Brief Report of Excavations of the Longshan Culture Site at Mengzhuang in Huixian City, Henan). *Kaogu* 3: 1-20.

———— (2000b) Henan Zhengzhou Shangcheng Gongdianqu Hangtuqiang 1998 Nian de Fajue (The 1998 Excavation of the Rammed-Earth Walls in the Palace Zone at the Zhengzhou Shang City, Henan). *Kaogu* 2: 40-60.

———— (2001) *Zhengzhou Shangcheng*. Wenwu Press, Beijing.

Hou, Dejun (1996) Shang Wangchao Shili de Nanxia yu Jiangnan Gutongkuang (The Southward Expansion of Shang Power and Ancient Copper Mines South of the Yangzi River). *Nanfang Wenwu* 1: 81-5.

Hua, Jueming (1999) *Zhongguo Gudai Jinshu Jishu: Tong He Tie Zaojiu de Wenming*. Daxiang Press, Zhengzhou.

Huangshi City Museum (1981) Hubei Tonglushan Chunqiu Shiqi

Bibliography

Liantong Yizhi Fajue Jianbao (Brief Report of Excavations of the Copper Smelting Site at Tonglushan in Hubei). *Wenwu* 8: 30-9.
—— (1984) Daye Guwenhua Yizhi Kaogu Diaocha (Archaeological Surveys of Ancient Sites in Daye). *Jianghan Kaogu* 4: 8-16.
—— (1999) *Tonglushan Gu Kuangye Yizhi (Ancient Mining and Smelting Sites at Tongludhan)*. Wenwu Press, Beijing.
Hubei Institute of Archaeology (2001) *Panlongcheng*. Wenwu, Beijing.
Hubei Provincial Museum (1976) Panlongcheng Shangdai Erligang Qi de Qingtongqi (Bronze Objects of the Erligang Phase of the Shang Dynasty at Panlongcheng). *Wenwu* 2: 26-41.
Hubei Provincial Museum, and Beijing University (1976) Panlongcheng Yi Jiu Qi Si Nian Tianye Kaogu Jiyao (Report of Archaeological Fieldwork at Panlongcheng in 1974). *Wenwu* 2: 5-15.
Hunan Institute of Archaeology (1992) Hunan Shimen Zaoshi Shangdai Yicun (Shang Remains at Zaoshi in Shimen, Hunan). *Kaogu Xuebao* 2: 185-220.
Hunan Institute of Archaeology (1999) *Hunan Kaogu Manbu*. Hunan Meishu Press, Changsha.
Hunan Provincial Bureau of Topography (1999) *Hunan Sheng Dituce*. Hunan Ditu Press, Changsha.
Hunan Provincial Museum (1985) Hunan Mayang Zhanguo Gutongkuang Qingli Jianbao (Brief Report of Excavation at Copper Mines of the Warring States Period in Mayang, Hunan). *Kaogu* 2: 113-23.
Huo, Youguang (1993) Shitan Luonan Hongyanshan Gutongkuang Cai Ye Di (in Search of Ancient Mining and Smelting Locations in Mt Hongyan in Luonan). *Kaogu yu Wenwu* 1: 94-7.
Inner Mongolia Institute of Cultural Relics (1988) Neimenggu Zhukaigou Yizhi (The Zhukaigou Site in Inner Mongolia). *Kaogu Xuebao* 3: 301-31.
—— (1990) Neimenggu Zhungeer Meitian Heidaigou Kuangqu Wenwu Pucha Shuyao (Surveys in the Heidaigou Coal Mining Area in Zhungeer, Inner Mongolia). *Kaogu* 1: 1-10, 55.
Inner Mongolia Institute of Cultural Relics, and Ordos Museum (2000) *Zhukaigou: Qingtong Shidai Zaoqi Yizhi Fajue Baogao*. Wenwu Press, Beijing.
Institute of Archaeology, CASS (1989) Jinnan Kaogu Diaocha Baogao (Report of Archaeological Surveys in Southern Shanxi). *Kaoguxue Jikan* 6: 1-51.
—— (1991) *Zhongguo Kaoguxue Zhong Tan Shisi Niandai Shujuji*. Wenwu Press, Beijing.
—— (1993) *Kaogu Jinghua*. Kexue Press, Beijing.
—— (1995) *Erlitou Taoqi Jicui*. Zhongguo Shehui Kexue Press, Beijing.

Bibliography

——— (1999) *Yanshi Erlitou.* Zhongguo Dabaikequanshu Press, Beijing.

Institute of Archaeology, CASS, National Museum of Chinese History and Shanxi Institute of Archaeology (1988) *Xiaxian Dongxiafeng.* Wenwu Press, Beijing.

Jiangxi Institute of Cultural Relics (1997) *Xingan Shangdai Damu.* Wenwu Press, Beijing.

Jiangxi Institute of Cultural Relics, and Ruichang Museum (2000) Jiangxi Ruichangshi Zhangshuzui Shang Zhou Yizhi Fajue Jianbao (Brief Report of Excavation at the Zhangshuzui Shang and Zhou Site in Ruichang City, Jiangxi). *Kaogu* 12: 50-9.

Jiangxi Institute of Cultural Relics, and Ruichang Museum (eds) (1997) *Tongling Gu Tongkuang Yizhi Faxian yu Yanjiu.* Jiangxi Kexue Jishu Press, Nanchang.

Jiangxi Institute of Cultural Relics, Xiamen University, and Zhangshu Museum (1995) Jiangxi Zhangshu Wucheng Shangdai Yizhi Dibaci Fajue Jianbao (Brief Report of the Eighth Season of Excavation of the Shang Site at Wucheng in Zhangshu, Jiangxi). *Nanfang Wenwu* 1: 5-21.

Jiangxi Provincial Cultural Relics Team (1987) Qingjiang Wucheng Yizhi Diliuci Fajue de Zhuyao Shouhuo (Major Gains of the Sixth Excavation at the Wucheng Site in Qingjiang). *Jiangxi Lishi Wenwu* 2: 20-31.

Jiangxi Provincial Cultural Relics Team, and Wannian Museum (1989) Jiangxi Wannian Leixing Shang Wenhua Yizhi Diaocha (Surveys of the Shang Sites of the Wannian Variant in Jiangxi). *Dongnan Wenhua* 4-5: 26-37.

Jiangxi Museum, and Qingjiang Museum (1975) Jiangxi Qingjiang Wucheng Yizhi Fajue Jianbao (Brief Report of Excavations of the Shang Site at Wucheng in Qingjiang, Jiangxi). *Wenwu* 7: 51-71.

——— (1978) Jiangxi Qingjiang Wucheng Shangdai Yizhi Disici Fajue de Zhuyao Shouhuo (Major Gains from the Fourth Season of Excavations of the Shang Site at Wucheng in Qingjiang, Jiangxi). In *Wenwu Ziliao Congkan*, pp. 1-14.

Jin, Jingfang and Shaogang Lu (1996) *'Shangshu, Yuxiashu' Xinjie.* Liaoning Guji Press, Shenyang.

Jin, Zhengyao (1987) Wan Shang Zhongyuan Qingtong de Kuangliao Laiyuan Yanjiu (Study of Alloy Provenances of the Late Shang Bronzes in the Central Plains). In *Kexueshi Lunji*, pp. 365-86. Zhongguo Keji Daxue Press, Hefei.

——— (2000) Erlitou Qingtongqi de Ziran Kexue Yanjiu yu Xia Wenming Tansuo (Scientific Studies of the Erlitou Bronzes and Xia Civilization). *Wenwu* 1: 56-64.

Jin, Zhengyao, W.T. Chase, Hirao Yoshimitsu, Mabuchi Hisao, Xizhang Yang and Miwa Karoku (1998) Zhongguo Lianghe Liuyu Qingtong

161

Bibliography

Wenming Zhijian de Lianxi (Relationships between Bronze Civilizations in the Two River Valleys in China). In *Zhongguo Shang Wenhua Guoji Xueshu Taolunhui Lunwenji*, edited by Institute of Archaeology, CASS, pp. 425-33. Zhongguo Dabaikequanshu Press, Beijing.

Jin, Zhengyao, W.T. Chase, Hirao Yoshimitsu, Shifan Peng, Mabuchi Hisao, Miwa Karoku and Kaixun Zhan (1994) Jiangxi Xingan Dayangzhou Shang Mu Qingtongqi de Qian Tongweisu Bizhi Yanjiu (A Study of the Ratios of Lead Isotope in Bronzes from the Shang Tomb at Dayangzhou, Xingan). *Kaogu* 8: 744-7.

Jin, Zhengyao, Mabuchi Hisao, Tom Chase, De'an Chen, Miwa Karoku, Hirao Yoshimitsu and Dianzeng Zhao (1995) Guanghan Sanxingdui Yiwukeng Qingtongqi de Qian Tongweisu Bizhi Yanjiu (A Study of the Ratios of Lead Isotpe in Bronzes from the Sanxingdui Pit-Burials). *Wenwu* 2: 80-5.

Jing, Zhichun and George (Rip) Rapp (1995) Holocene Landscape Evolution and Its Impact on the Neolithic and Bronze Age Sites in the Shangqiu Area, Northern China. *Geoarchaeology: An International Journal* 10: 481-513.

Jingzhou Museum (1989) Hubei Jiangling Jingnansi Yizhi Diyierci Fajue Jianbao (Brief Report of the First and Second Seasons of Excavation at Jingnansi in Jiangling, Hubei). *Kaogu* 8: 679-92, 98.

Jinzhong Archeology Team (1989) Shanxi Taigu Baiyan Yizhi Diyi Didian Fajue Jianbao (Brief Report of Excavation of Locality 1 at the Baiyan Site in Taigu, Shanxi). *Wenwu* 3: 1-21.

Johnson, Gregory (1973) Local Exchange and Early State Development in Southwestern Iran. *Museum of Anthropology, University of Michigan Anthropological Papers* 51.

—— (1977) Aspect of Regional Analysis in Archaeology. *Annual Review of Anthropology* 6: 479-508.

—— (1981) Monitoring Complex System Integration and Boundary Phenomena with Settlement Size Data. In *Archaeological Approaches to the Study of Complexity*, edited by Sander E. van der Leeuw, pp. 143-88. A.E. van Giffen Instituut woor Prae- en Protohistorie, Amsterdam.

—— (1987) The Changing Organization of Uruk Administration on the Susiana Plain. In *The Archaeology of Western Iran: Settlement and Society from Prehistory to the Islamic Conquest*, edited by Frank Hole, pp. 107-40. Smithsonian Institution Press, Washington DC.

Keightley, David (1979-80) The Shang State as Seen in the Oracle-Bone Inscriptions. *Early China* 5: 25-34.

—— (1983) The Late Shang State: When, Where, and What? In *The Origins of Chinese Civilization*, edited by David Keightley, pp. 523-64. University of California Press, Berkeley.

———— (1999) The Shang: China's First Historical Dynasty. In *The Cambridge History of Ancient China: From the Origins of Civilization to 221 BC*, edited by Michael Loewe and Edward L. Shaughnessy, pp. 232-91. Cambridge University Press, Cambridge.

———— (2000) *The Ancestral Landscape: Time, Space, and Community in Late Shang China*. Institute of East Asian Studies, Berkeley.

Kipp, R. and E. Schortman (1989) The Political Impact of Trade in Chiefdoms. *American Anthropologist* 91: 370-85.

Kowalewski, Stephen A. (1982) The Evolution of Primate Regional Systems. *Comparative Urban Research* 9: 60-78.

Lei, Xingshan (2000) Dui Guanzhong Diqu Shang Wenhua de Jidian Renshi (On the Shang Culture in the Central Shaanxi Region). *Kaogu yu Wenwu* 2: 28-34.

Li, Boqian (1983) Chenggu Tongqiqun yu Zaoqi Shu Wenhua (The Bronze Assemblage from Chenggu and the Early Shu Culture). *Kaogu yu Wenwu* 2: 66-70.

———— (1989) Xian Shang Wenhua Tansuo (In Search of the Proto-Shang Culture). In *Qingzhu Su Bingqi Kaogu Wushiwu Nian Lunwenji*, edited by 'Qingzhu Su Bingqi Kaogu Wushiwu Nian Lunwenji' Editorial Board, pp. 280-93. Wenwu Press, Beijing.

Li, Jiahe, Juyuan Yang and Shizhong Liu (1990) Jiangxi Wannian Leixing Shang Wenhua Yanjiu (The Wannian Variant of the Shang Culture in Jiangxi). *Dongnan Wenhua* 3: 142-60.

Li, Jinghua (1985) Guanyu Zhongyuan Diqu Zaoqi Yetong Jishu Ji Xiangguan Wenti de Jidian Kanfa (Some Thoughts on Early Bronze Metallurgy in the Central Plains). *Wenwu* 12: 75-8.

Li, Keyou and Shifan Peng (1975) Luelun Jiangxi Wucheng Shangdai Yuanshi Ciqi (On the Primitive Porcelain Wares of the Shang Dynasty from Wucheng in Jiangxi). *Wenwu* 7: 77-82.

Li, Wenjie (1996) *Zhongguo Gudai Zhitao Gongyi Yanjiu*. Kexue Press, Beijing.

Li, Xueqin (1997a) Tan Changjiang Liuyu de Shangdai Qingtong Wenhua (On the Shang Bronze Culture in the Yangzi River Valley). In *Bijiao Kaoguxue Suibi*, edited by Xueqin Li, pp. 178-86. Guangxi Shifan Daxue Press, Guilin.

———— (ed.) (1997b) *Zhongguo Gudai Wenming yu Guojia Xingcheng Yanjiu*. Yunnan Renmin Press, Kunming.

———— (1999) Rongsheng Bianzhong Lunshi (Interpretation of the Rongsheng Bell Set). *Wenwu* 9: 75-82.

Li, Yanxiang (1993) Zhongtiaoshan Gu Tongkuangye Yizhi Chubu Kaocha Yanjiu (Preliminary Investigation and Research of Ancient Copper Mining Sites in the Zhongtiao Mountains). *Wenwu Jikan* 2: 64-7.

Lin, Yun (1998) Jiaguwen Zhong de Shangdai Fangguo Lianmeng (The Confederation States of the Shang Dynasty Seen in Oracle-Bone

163

Inscriptions) (originally published in 1982 *Guwenzi Yanjiu 6*). In *Lin Yun Xueshu Wenji*, edited by Yun Lin, pp. 69-84. Zhongguo Dabaike Quanshu Press, Beijing.

Linduff, Katheryn (1998) The Emergence and Demise of Bronze-Producing Cultures Outside the Central Plain of China. In *The Bronze Age and Early Iron Age Peoples of Eastern Central Asia*, edited by Victor H. Mair, pp. 619-46. Institute for the Study of Man Inc., Washington DC.

―――― (2000) Introduction. In *The Beginnings of Metallurgy in China*, edited by Katheryn M. Linduff, Rubin Han and Shuyun Sun, pp. 1-28. Edwin Mellen Press, New York.

Linduff, Katheryn and Emma Bunker (1997) An Archaeological Overview. In *Ancient Bronzes of the Eastern Eurasian Steppes from the Arthur M. Sackler Collections*, edited by Emma Bunker, Trudy Kawami, Katheryn Linduff and Wu En, pp. 18-32. Arthur M. Sackler Foundation, New York.

Liu, Jianzhou (1981) Gongxian Tangsancai Yaozhi Diaocha (Surveys of the Tang Dynasty Three-Coloured Ceramic Kilns in Gongyi). *Zhongyuan Wenwu* 3: 16-22.

Liu, Li (1996a) Mortuary Ritual and Social Hierarchy in the Longshan Culture. *Early China* 21: 1-46.

―――― (1996b) Settlement Patterns, Chiefdom Variability, and the Development of Early States in North China. *Journal of Anthropological Archaeology* 15: 237-88.

―――― (2000) The Development and Decline of Social Complexity in China: Some Environmental and Social Factors. *Indo-Pacific Prehistory: The Melaka Papers. Bulletin of the Indo-Pacific Prehistory Association* 20(4): 14-33.

―――― (2003) Production of Prestige Goods in the Neolithic and Early State Periods of China. *Asian Perspectives* 42(1): 1-40.

―――― (forthcoming) Urbanization in China: Erlitou and Its Hinterland. In *Population and Preindustrial Cities: A Cross-Cultural Perspective*, edited by Glann Storey. University of Alabama Press, Tuscaloosa.

Liu, Li and Xingcan Chen (2000) Cheng: Xia Shang Shiqi Dui Ziran Ziyuan de Kongzhi Wenti (Cities: Control of Natural Resources in the Xia and Shang Period). *Dongnan Wenhua* 3: 45-60.

―――― (2001a) China. In *Encyclopedia of Archaeology: History and Discoveries*, edited by Tim Murray, pp. 315-33. ABC-CLIO, Santa Barbara.

―――― (2001b) Cities and Towns: The Control of Natural Resources in Early States, China. *Bulletin of the Museum of Far Eastern Antiquities* 73: 5-550.

Liu, Shizhong and Benshan Lu (1997) Ruichang Shi Tongling Tongkuang Yizhi Fajue Baogao (Report of Excavations at the

Tongling Mining Site in Ruicheng). In *Tongling Gu Tongkuang Yizhi Faxian yu Yanjiu*, edited by Jiangxi Institute of Cultural Relics and Ruichang Museum. Jiangxi Kexue Jishu Press, Nanchang.

────── (1998) Jiangxi Tongling Tongkuang Yizhi de Fajue yu Yanjiu (Excavation and Study of the Copper Mining Site at Tongling, Jiangxi). *Kaogu Xuebao* 4: 465-96.

Liu, Xu (1990) Lun Wei Huai Diqu de Xia Shang Wenhua (On the Xia and Shang Culture in the Wei and Huai Regions). In *Jinian Beijing Daxue Kaogu Zhuanye Sanshi Zhounian Lunwenji*, pp. 171-210. Wenwu Press, Beijing.

Long, Qing, Jian Bai and Yuan Ju (1992) Jiangxi Zao Shang Wenhua Yicun de Faxian yu Yanjiu (Discovery and Study of the Early-Shang Remains in Jiangxi). *Dongnan Wenhua* 3-4: 82-92.

Longacre, W.A. (1999) Standardization and Specialization: What's the Link? In *Pottery and People: A Dynamic Interaction*, edited by J. Skibo and G. Feinman, pp. 4-58. University of Utah Press, Salt Lake City.

Lu, Benshan and Shizhong Liu (1997) Tongling Shang Zhou Tongkuang Kaicai Jishu Chubu Yanjiu (Preliminary Study of the Mining Techniques Used in Shang and Zhou Copper Mines at Tongling). In *Tongling Gu Tongkuang Yizhi Faxian yu Yanjiu*, edited by Jiangxi Institute of Cultural Relics and Ruichang Museum, pp. 118-21. Jiangxi Kexue Jishu Press, Nanchang.

Luo, Renlin (1999) Yueyang Diqu Shang Shiqi de Wenhua Xulie Jiqi Wenhua Yinsu Fenxi (Analysis of Cultural Elements and Chronology in the Shang Period in the Yueyang Region). *Hunan Kaogu Jikan* 7: 223-51.

Maceachern, Scott (1998) Scale, Style, and Cultural Variation: Technological Traditions in the Northern Mandara Mountains. In *The Archaeology of Social Boundaries*, edited by Miriam Stark, pp. 107-31. Smithsonian Institution Press, Washington and London.

Maisels, Charles (1987) Models of Social Evolution: Trajectories from the Neolithic to the State. *Man* 22: 331-59.

────── (1990) *The Emergence of Civilization: From Hunting and Gathering to Agriculture, Cities, and the State in the Near East*. Routledge, London.

Marcus, Joyce and Gary Feinman (1998) Introduction. In *Archaic States*, edited by Gary Feinman and Joyce Marcus, pp. 3-14. School of American Research Press, Santa Fe.

Marx, K.H., (1973) *Grundrisse: Foundations of the Critique of Political Economy*. Penguin, Harmondsworth.

Meng, Wentong (1998) Nan Xia Shuidao Jiaotong (Water Transport Routes to the South). In *Gudi Zhenwei*, edited by Wentong Meng, pp. 12-13. Bashu Press, Chengdu.

Meng, Xianmin and Lihua Zhao (1985) Quanguo Jianxuan Wenwu

Bibliography

Zhanlan Xunli (Exhibition of Nation-Wide Selected Cultural Relics). *Wenwu* 1: 66-71.

Muhly, James D. (1988) The Beginnings of Metallurgy in the Old World. In *The Beginning of the Use of Metals and Alloys*, edited by Robert Maddin, pp. 2-20. MIT Press, Cambridge, Mass.

Murowchick, Robert and David Cohen (2001) Searching for Shang's Beginnings: Great City Shang, City Song, and Collaborative Archaeology in Shangqui, Henan. *Review of Archaeology* 22: 47-60.

National Museum of Chinese History and Shanxi Institute of Archaeology (1996) *Yuanqu Shangcheng: 1985-1986 Niandu Kancha Baogao*. Kexue Press, Beijing.

Nichols, Deborah L. and Thomas H. Charlton (1997) *The Archaeology of City-States: Cross-Cultural Approaches*. Smithsonian Institution Press, Washington DC.

Pei, Mingxiang (1993) Zhengzhou Shangdai Wangcheng de Buju Jiqi Wenhua Neihan (Plan and Cultural Remains of the Shang Capital at Zhengzhou). In *Zhengzhou Shangcheng Kaogu Xinfaxian yu Yanjiu*, edited by Henan Institute of Cultural Relics, pp. 7-14. Zhongzhou Guji Press, Zhengzhou.

Peng, Ke and Yanshi Zhu (1999) Zhongguo Gudai Suoyong Haibei Laiyuan Xintan (New Inquiry in the Sources of Cowries in Ancient China). *Kaoguxue Jikan* 12: 119-47.

Peng, Shifan (1987) *Zhongguo Nanfang Gudai Yinwentao*. Wenwu Press, Beijing.

—— (1999) Wenbu Qianjin Shuoguo Leilei – Jiangxi Kaogu Wushi Nian (Progress and Achievement – Fifty Years of Archaeology in Jiangxi). *Nanfang Wenwu* 3: 16-28.

Potts, Daniel (1984) On Salt and Salt Gathering in Ancient Mesopotamia. *Journal of the Economic and Social History of the Orient* XXVII: 225-71.

Railey, Jim (1999) *Neolithic to Early Bronze Age Sociopolitical Evolution in the Yuanqu Basin, North-Central China*. PhD dissertation, Washington University, Saint Louis.

Rice, Prudence M. (1981) Evolution of Specialized Pottery Production: A Trial Model. *Current Anthropology* 22: 219-40.

—— (1996) Recent Ceramic Analysis: 2. Composition, Production and Theory. *Journal of Archaeological Research* 4: 165-202.

Santley, Robert and Rani Alexander (1992) The Political Economy of Core-Periphery Systems. In *Resources, Power, and Inter-Regional Interaction*, edited by Edward Schortman and Patricia Urban, pp. 23-49. Plenum, New York.

Shandong Bureau of Cultural Relics Management (1974) *Dawenkou*. Wenwu Press, Beijing.

Shandong Institute of Cultural Relics and Archaeology (1989) Qingzhou Shi Fenghuangtai Yizhi Fajue (Excavations at the

Bibliography

Fenghuangtai Site in Qingzhou City). In *Haidai Kaogu (I)*, edited by Xuehai Zhang, pp. 141-82. Shandong Daxue Press, Jinan.

Shandong University (1992) Shandong Zouping Dinggong Yizhi Diersanci Fajue Jianbao (Brief Report of the Second and Third Seasons of Excavations at the Dinggong Site in Zouping, Shandong). *Kaogu* 6: 496-504.

Shaughnessy, Edward L. (1989) Historical Geography and the Extent of the Earliest Chinese Kingdoms. *Asia Major* 11: 1-22.

Shelach, Gideon (1996) The Qiang and the Question of Human Sacrifice in the Late Shang Period. *Asian Perspectives* 35: 1-26.

Shih, Chang-ju (1955) Yindai de Zhutong Gongyi (Bronze Metallurgy in the Yin Dynasty). *Bulletin of the Institute of History and Philology, Academia Sinica* 26: 95-129.

Shima, Kunio (1958) *Inkyo Bokuji Kenkyu*. Kyuko Shoin, Tokyo.

Sino-American Huan River Valley Archaeology Team (1998) Huanhe Liuyu Kaogu Yanjiu Chubu Baogao (Preliminary Report of Regional Archaeological Research in the Huan River Valley). *Kaogu* 10: 13-22.

Skinner, William (1977) Cities and the Hierarchy of Local Systems. In *The City in Late Imperial China*, edited by William Skinner, pp. 276-351. Stanford University Press, Stanford.

Song, Guoding (1993) 1985-92 Nian Zhengzhou Shangcheng Kaogu Faxian Zongshu (Summary of Archaeological Discoveries at the Zhengzhou Shang City from 1985 to 1992). In *Zhengzhou Shangcheng Kaogu Xinfaxian yu Yanjiu*, edited by Henan Institute of Cultural Relics, pp. 48-59. Zhongzhou Guji Press, Zhengzhou.

Song, Guoding and Xinhua Jiang (2000) Zhengzhou Shangdai Yizhi Baofen Yu Guisuanti Fenxi Baogao (Analysis on Pollen and Phytoliths in the Zhengzhou Area of the Shang Dynasty). In *Huanjing Kaogu Yanjiu*, edited by Kunshu Zhou and Yuqin Song, pp. 180-7. Kexue Press, Beijing.

Song, Huanwen (1983) Cong Panlongcheng Kaogu Faxian Shitan Shang Chu Guanxi (On the Relationship between Shang and Chu Based on Archaeological Finds at Panlongcheng). *Jianghan Kaogu* 2: 61-5.

Song, Jian (2000) Maqiao Wenhua Yuanshi Ci He Yinwen Tao Yanjiu (On Proto-Porcelain and Stamped Ceramics in the Maqiao Culture). *Wenwu* 3: 45-53.

Song, Xinchao (1987) Xi'an Laoniupo Yizhi Fajue de Zhuyao Shouhuo (Major Gains in the Excavations at the Laoniupo Site in Xi'an). *Xibei Daxue Xuebao* 1: 44-6.

—— (1991) *Yin Shang Wenhua Quyu Yanjiu*. Shaanxi Renmin Press, Xi'an.

—— (1992) Shilun Laoniupo Shang Wenhua Fenqi Ji Tezheng (Periodization and Characteristics of the Shang Culture at Laoniupo). *Wenbo* 2: 12-18, 41.

Southall, Aidan (1956) *Alur Society: A Study in Processes and Types of Domination.* Heffer, Cambridge.

—— (1988) The Segmentary State in Africa and Asia. *Comparative Studies in Society and History* 30: 52-82.

—— (1991) The Segmentary State: From the Imaginary to the Material Means of Production. In *Early State Economics*, edited by H.J.M. Claessen and P. van de Velde. Transaction Publishers, New Brunswick.

—— (1993) Urban Theory and the Chinese City. In *Urban Anthropology in China*, edited by G. Guldin and A. Southall, pp. 19-40. E.J. Brill, Leiden.

—— (1999) The Segmentary State and the Ritual Phase in Political Economy. In *Beyond Chiefdoms: Pathways to Complexity in Africa*, edited by Susan K. McIntosh, pp. 31-8. Cambridge University Press, Cambridge.

Stein, Burton (1977) The Segmentary State in South Indian History. In *Realm and Region in Traditional India*, edited by R.G. Fox. Duke University Press, Durham, NC.

—— (1980) *Peasant, State and Society in Medieval South India.* Oxford University Press, Delhi.

Stein, Gil (1999) *Rethinking World-Systems: Diasporas, Colonies, and Interaction in Uruk Mesopotamia.* University of Arizona Press, Tucson.

Steponaitis, Vincas (1981) Settlement Hierarchy and Political Complexity in Nonmarket Societies: The Formative Period of the Valley of Mexico. *American Anthropologist* 83: 320-63.

Steward, C.T. (1958) The Size and Spacing of Cities. *Geographical Review* 48: 222-45.

Sun, Yirang (1987 edition) *Zhouli Zhengyi.* Zhonghua Press, Beijing.

Sung, Ying-hsing (1966) *T'ien-Kung K'ai-Wu: Chinese Technology in the Seventeenth Century* [original text 1637]. Pennsylvania State University Press, University Park and London.

Tambiah, Stanley Jeyaraja (1977) The Galactic Polity: The Structure of Traditional Kingdoms in Southeast Asia. In *Anthropology and the Climate of Opinion*, edited by Stanley Freed, pp. 69-97. New York Academy of Sciences, New York.

—— (1985) *Culture, Thought, and Social Action: An Anthropological Perspective.* Harvard University Press, Cambridge.

Tan, Qixiang (1981) Xihan Yiqian de Huanghe Xiayou Hedao (The Yellow River's Lower Courses before the Western Han). *Lishi Dili* 1: 48-64.

—— (ed.) (1982) *Zhongguo Lishi Dituji – Yuanshi Shehui, Xia,*

Bibliography

Shang, Xizhou, Chunqiu, Zhanguo Shiqi. Zhongguo Ditu Press, Beijing.

Tang, J., Z. Jing and G. Rapp (2000) The Largest Walled Shang City Located in Anyang, China. *Antiquity* 74: 479-80.

Tang, Jigen (1999) Zhong Shang Wenhua Yanjiu (Study of the Middle Shang Culture). *Kaogu Xuebao* 4: 393-420.

—— (2001) The Construction of an Archaeological Chronology for the History of the Shang Dynasty of Early Bronze Age China. *Review of Archaeology* 22: 35-47.

Thorp, Robert (1991) Erlitou and the Search for the Xia. *Early China* 16: 1-38.

Tong, Weihua (1998) Shangdai Qianqi Yuanqu Pendi de Tongzhi Zhongxin – Yuanqu Shangcheng (the Early-Shang Political Center in the Yuanqu Basin – Yuanqu Shang Town). *Zhongguo Lishi Bowuguan Guankan* 1: 89-100.

Trigger, Bruce (1993) *Early Civilizations: Ancient Egypt in Context.* American University in Cairo Press, Cairo.

—— (1999) Shang Political Organization: A Comparative Approach. *Journal of East Asian Archaeology* 1: 43-62.

Tylecote, R.F. (1976) *A History of Metallurgy.* The Metals Society, London.

Wang, Changfu and Yachang Yang (1997) Shangzhou Faxian Yichu Daxing Xia Shang Yizhi (Discovery of a Large Xia-Shang Site in Shangzhou). In *Zhongguo Wenwubao*, 26 October, Beijing.

Underhill, Anne (1994) Variation in Settlements during the Longshan Period of Northern China. *Asian Perspectives* 33: 197-228.

Wang, Chuanlei, Mingsong Qi and Yongtao Li (1998) Panlongcheng Shangdai Chengzhi Tianye Kaogu Wutan Gongzuo Zongjie (Results of Archaeological Remote Sensing at the Panlongcheng Shang Town). *Jianghan Kaogu* 3: 49-52.

Wang, Jin and Xianyi Chen (1987) Shilun Shangdai Panlongcheng Zaoqi Chengshi de Xingtai yu Tezheng (On the Form and Characteristics of the Early City at Panlongcheng). In *Hubeisheng Kaoguxuehui Lunwen Xuanji*, edited by Hubei Archaeology Association, pp. 70-7. Wuhan Daxue Press, Wuhan.

Wang, Lixin (1998) *Zao Shang Wenhua Yanjiu.* Gaodeng Jiaoyu Press, Beijing.

Wang, Lizhi (1999a) Donglongshan Yizhi Fajue de Yiyi Yiji Shouhuo (Significance and Gains from Excavations at the Donglongshan Site). *Qingnian Kaogu Xuejia* 11: 30-1.

Wang, Ningsheng (2002) 'Xiaochen' Zhi Chengwei Youlai Ji Shenfen (Meaning and Status of 'Xiaochen'). *Huaxia Kaogu* 1: 56-60.

Wang, Wenchu (1996) Lishi Shiqi Nanyang Pendi yu Zhongyuan Diqu Jian de Jiaotong Fazhan (The Development of Transportation between the Nanyang Basin and the Central Plains During Historical

Bibliography

Times). In *Gudai Jiaotong Dili Congkao*, edited by Wenchu Wang, pp. 1-17. Zhonghua Press, Beijing.

Wang, Wenjian (1989) Shang Shiqi Lishui Liuyu Qingtong Wenhua de Xulie He Wenhua Yinsu Fenxi (Analyses of Chronology and Cultural Components of Bronze Cultures in the Li River Valley During the Shang Period). In *Kaogu Leixingxue de Lilun yu Shijian*, edited by Weichao Yu, pp. 110-44. Wenwu Press, Beijing.

Wang, Wenjian and Xibin Long (1987) Shimen Xian Shang Shiqi Yicun Diaocha – Baota Yizhi yu Weigang Muzang (Surveys of Sites in the Shang Period in Shimen County – the Baota Site and the Weigang Burial). *Hunan Kaogu Jikan* 4: 11-18.

Wang, Xuerong (1999b) Yanshi Shangcheng Buju de Tansuo He Sikao (Inquiry and Thoughts about the Plan of Yanshi Shang City). *Kaogu* 2: 24-34.

——— (2000) Henan Yanshi Shangcheng Di II Hao Jianzhuqun Yizhi Yanjiu (On the No. 2 Architectural Cluster at the Yanshi Shang City in Henan). *Huaxia Kaogu* 1: 41-60.

Wang, Youbang (1995) *Zhongguo Ziran Ziyuan Congshu: Shandong Juan*. Zhongguo Huanjing Kexue Press, Beijing.

Wang, Zengshan, Jianrong Li and Gongye Li (1997) Shandong Sichu Dongzhou Taoyao Yizhi de Diaocha (Survey of Four Kiln Sites of the Eastern Zhou in Shandong). *Kaoguxue Jikan* 11: 292-7.

Wang, Zeqing and Jishu Lu (1986) 'Yuanqu Dianxiayang' Jianshu (Preliminary Report of the 'Yuanqu Weight'). *Wenwu* 1: 78-9.

Wei, Si (1998) Tangdai de Hedong Yanchi (The Hedong Salt Lake in the Tang Dynasty). In *Wei Si Kaogu Lunwenji*, edited by Si Wei, pp. 192-5. Shanxi Guji Press, Taiyuan.

Welch, Paul (1991) *Moundville's Economy*. University of Alabama Press, Tuscaloosa.

Wheatley, Paul (1971) *The Pivot of the Four Quarters: A Preliminary Enquiry into the Origins and Character of the Ancient Chinese City*. Aldine Publishing Company, Chicago.

Wolf, Eric (1982) *Europe and the People without History*. University of California Press, Berkeley.

Wright, Henry (1977) Recent Research on the Origin of the State. *Annual Review of Anthropology* 6: 379-97.

——— (1984) Prestate Political Formations. In *On the Evolution of Complex Societies: Essays in Honor of Harry Hoijer*, edited by T. Earle, pp. 41-77. Undena Publication, Malibu.

——— (1986) The Evolution of Civilizations. In *American Archaeology Past and Future*, edited by David J. Meltzer, Don D. Fowler, and Jeremy A. Sabloff. Smithsonian Institution Press, Washington DC.

Wright, Henry and Gregory Johnson (1975) Population, Exchange, and Early State Formation in Southwestern Iran. *American Anthropologist* 77: 267-89.

Bibliography

Wuhan Museum (1998) 1997-98 Nian Panlongcheng Fajue Jianbao (Preliminary Report of Excavation at Panlongcheng in 1997-98). *Jianghan Kaogu* 3: 34-48.

Xia, Mingcai (1989) Qingzhou Shi Zhaopu Yizhi de Qingli (Excavation of the Zhaopu Site in Qingzhou City). In *Haidai Kaogu (1)*, edited by Xuehai Zhang, pp. 183-95. Shandong Daxue Press, Jinan.

Xia, Nai and Weizhang Yin (1982) Hubei Tonglushan Gutongkuang (Ancient Copper Mines at Tonglushang, Hubei). *Kaogu Xuebao* 1: 1-13.

Xia Shang Zhou Chronology Project Team (editor) (2000) *Xia Shang Zhou Duandai Gongcheng 1996-2000 Nian Jieduan Chengguo Baogao*. Shijie Tushu Press, Beijing.

Xia, Zongyong (1995) *Zhongguo Ziran Ziyuan Congshu: Henan Juan*. Zhongguo Huanjing Kexue Press, Beijing.

Xi'an Banpo Museum (1981) Shaanxi Lantian Huaizhenfang Shangdai Yizhi Shijue Jianbao. *Kaogu yu Wenwu* 3: 48-53.

Xiaxian County Chronicles Editorial Board (1998) *Xiaxian Zhi*. Renmin Press, Beijing.

Xibei University (1988) Xi'an Laoniupo Shangdai Mudi de Fajue (Excavation of the Shang Burial Site at Laoniupo in Xi'an). *Wenwu* 6: 1-22.

Xinyang Cultural Relics Management Bureau (1981a) Henan Luoshan Xian Mangzhang Shangdai Mudi Diyici Fajue Jianbao (Preliminary Report of the First Excavation of the Shang Burial Site at Mangzhang in Luoshan, Henan). *Kaogu* 2: 111-18.

—— (1981b) Luoshan Xian Mangzhang Houli Shang Zhou Mudi Dierci Fajue Jianbao (Preliminary Report of the Second Excavation of the Shang and Zhou Burial Site at Houli, Mangzhang, in Luoshan). *Zhongyuan Wenwu* 4: 4-13.

Xu, Changqing, Songling Weng and Jiahe Li (1994) Jiangxi Xia Wenhua Yicun de Faxian yu Yanjiu. *Nanfang Wenwu* 2: 54-66.

Xu, Ji (1994) Shang Wenhua Dongjian Chulun (On the Eastward Progression of the Shang Culture). *Nanfang Wenwu* 2: 8-13.

—— (1997) Shang Wenhua Daxinzhuang Leixing Chulun (Preliminary Study of the Daxinzhuang Type of the Shang Culture). In *Zhongguo Kaogu Xuehui Di Jiuci Nianhui Lunwenji*, edited by Chinese Archaeological Association, pp. 205-20. Wenwu Press, Beijing.

—— (1998a) Jinan Daxinzhuang Shangdai Wenhua Yicun de Zai Renshi (Rethinking the Shang Cultural Remains at Daxinzhuang, Jinan). In *Zhongguo Shang Wenhua Guoji Xueshu Taolunhui Lunwenji*, edited by Institute of Archaeology, CASS, pp. 265-81. Zhongguo Dabaikequanshu Press, Beijing.

Xu, Junping and Feng Li (1997) Xiaoshuangqiao Shangdai Yizhi Xing-

Bibliography

zhi Tansuo (On the Nature of the Xiaoshuangqiao Site in the Shang Dynasty). *Zhongyuan Wenwu* 3: 106-10.

Xu, Lianggao (1998b) Wenhua Yinsu Dingxing Fenxi yu Shangdai 'Qingtong Liqi Wenhua Quan' Yanjiu (An Analysis of Cultural Elements and 'Cultural Sphere of Bronze Ritual Vessels'). In *Zhongguo Shang Wenhua Guoji Xueshu Taolunhui Lunwenji*, edited by Institute of Archaeology, CASS, pp. 227-36. Zhongguo Dabaike Quanshu Press, Beijing.

Yang, Hongxun (2001) *Gongdian Kaogu Tonglun*. Zijincheng Press, Beijing.

Yang, Lixin (1991a) Wannan Gudai Tongkuang de Faxian Jiqi Lishi Jiazhi (Historical Significance of the Discovery of the Ancient Copper Mines in Southern Anhui). *Dongnan Wenhua* 2: 131-7.

———— (1998) Tongling Gudai Tongye Shelue (On Ancient Copper Smelting at Tongling). *Wenwu Yanjiu* 11: 238-45.

Yang, Nan (2000a) Lun Shang Zhou Shiqi Yuanshi Ciqi de Quyu Tezheng (Regional Characteristics of Protoporcelain in the Shang and Zhou Periods). *Wenwu* 3: 54-62.

Yang, Shengnan (1986) Yin Ren Luqian Bianxi (Analysis of Moving Capitals of the Yin). In *Jiaguwen yu Yin Shang Shi*, edited by Houxuan Hu, pp. 185-222. Shanghai Guji Press, Shanghai.

———— (1992) *Shangdai Jingjishi*. Guizhou Renmin Press, Guiyang.

Yang, Xizhang, and Jigen Tang (1999) Yubei Jinan Diqu de Zhong Shang Yicun yu Pan Geng Yiqian de Shangdu Qianxi (The Middle Shang Remains in the Northern Henan and Southern Hebei Region and the Move of Capitals Prior to Pan Geng). In *Sandai Wenming Yanjiu*, edited by Three Dynasties Civilization Editorial Board, pp. 248-56. Kexue Press, Beijing.

Yang, Yachang (2000b) Shaanxi Xia Shiqi Kaogu de Xin Jinzhan (New Progress of the Xia Archaeology in Shaanxi). *Gudai Wenming Yanjiu Tongbao* 5: 34-6.

Yang, Yubin (1964) Henan Yanshi Yangshao Ji Shangdai Yizhi (Yangshao and Shang Dynasty Sites in Yanshi, Henan). *Kaogu* 3: 161-2.

———— (1991b) *Zhonguo Wenwu Dituji: Henan Fence*. Zhongguo Ditu Press, Beijing.

Yanshi County Chronicle Editorial Board (1992) *Yanshi Xianzhi*. Sanlian Press, Beijing.

Yates, Robin (1997) The City-State in Ancient China. In *The Archaeology of City-States: Cross-Cultural Approaches*, edited by Deborah Nichols and Thomas Charlton, pp. 71-90. Smithsonian Institution Press, Washington DC.

You, Qinghan (1956) Zhengzhou Shi Minggonglu Xice Faxian Shangdai Zhitao Gongchang, Fangji Deng Yizhi (Discoveries of Ceramic Workshops and House Foundations of the Shang Dynasty at Western Minggonglu, Zhengzhou). *Wenwu* 1: 64.

Yuan, Guangkuo (2002) Guanyu Zhengzhou Shangcheng Waiguocheng de Jige Wenti (Issues Relating to the Outer Wall of the Zhengzhou Shang City). *Gudai Wenming Yanjiu Tongxun* 11: 7-15.

Yuan, Guangkuo and Xiaoli Qin (2000) Henan Jiaozuo Fucheng Yizhi Fajue Baogao. *Kaogu Xuebao* 4: 501-36.

Yuan, Guangkuo, Xiaoli Qin and Guijin Yang (2000) Henan Jiaozuo Shi Fucheng Yizhi Fajue Jianbao (Brief Report of Excavations at Fucheng in Jiaozuo, Henan). *Huaxia Kaogu* 2: 16-35.

Yue, Hongbin (1995) Yanshixian Erlitou Yizhi (The Erlitou Site at Yanshi County). In *Zhongguo Kaoguxue Nianjian*, edited by Chinese Archaeology Association, pp. 163-4. Wenwu Press, Beijing.

Zhang, Changshou and Kwang-chih Chang (1997) Henan Shangqiu Diqu Yin Shang Wenming Diaocha Fajue Chubu Baogao (Preliminary Report of Surveys and Excavations of the Shang Civilization in the Shangqiu Area in Henan). *Kaogu* 4: 24-31.

Zhang, Guomao (1991) Anhui Tongling Diqu Xian Qin Qingtong Wenhua Jianlun (On the Pre-Qin Bronze Culture in the Tongling Region, Anhui). *Dongnan Wenhua* 2: 138-44.

—— (1999a) Anhui Tongling Gudai Tongkuang Kaicai yu Yelian (Ancient Copper Mining and Smelting at Tongling in Anhui). In *Qingtong Wenhua Yanjiu*, edited by Chengyuan Ma, pp. 124-35. Huangshan Press, Hefei.

Zhang, Guowei (1989a) Shanxi Wenxi Guwenhua Yizhi Diaocha Jianbao (Preliminary Report on Surveys of Ancient Sites in Wenxi, Shanxi). *Kaogu* 3: 200-17.

Zhang, Kui (1995) *Zhongguo Ziran Ziyuan Congshu: Shanxi Juan*. Zhongguo Ziran Kexue Press, Beijing.

Zhang, Lidong (1996) Lun Huiwei Wenhua (on the Huiwei Culture). *Kaoguxue Jikan* 10: 206-56.

—— (1999b) Xian Shang Wenhua de Tansuo Licheng (In Search of the Proto-Shang Culture). In *Sandai Wenming Yanjiu*, edited by The Three Dynasties Civilization Editorial Board, pp. 200-7. Kexue Press, Beijing.

Zhang, Tian'en (1998) Shaanxi Shang Zhou Kaogu Faxian He Yanjiu Gaishu (Brief Summary of Discoveries and Research of Shang and Zhou Archaeology in Shaanxi). *Kaogu yu Wenwu* 5: 21-31.

—— (2000) Guanzhong Xibu Xiadai Wenhua Yicun de Tansuo (In Search of the Cultural Remains of the Xia Dynasty in Western Central Shaanxi). *Kaogu yu Wenwu* 3: 44-50, 84.

Zhang, Wenjun, Yushi Zhang and Yanming Fang (1993) Guanyu Zhengzhou Shangcheng de Kaoguxue Niandai Jiqi Ruogan Wenti (Issues Relating to Archaeological Chronology of the Zhengzhou Shang City). In *Zhengzhou Shangcheng Kaogu Xinfaxian yu Yanjiu*, edited by Henan Institute of Cultural Relics, pp. 30-47. Zhongzhou Guji Press, Zhengzhou.

173

Bibliography

Zhang, Xuehai (1989b) Lun Sishi Nianlai Shandong Xian Qin Kaogu de Jiben Shouhuo (On the Major Achievement of Pre-Qin Archaeology in Shandong in the Recent 40 Years). In *Haidai Kaogu*, edited by Xuehai Zhang, pp. 325-43. Shandong Daxue Press, Jinan.

Zhang, Zaiming, Jin Xu and Jianming Qin (1999) *Zhongguo Wenwu Dituji: Shaanxi Fence*. Xi'an Ditu Press, Xi'an.

Zhangjiakou Archaeology Team (1982) Yuxian Kaogu Jilue (Brief Report of Archaeology in Yuxian). *Kaogu yu Wenwu* 4: 10-14.

—— (1984) Yuxian Xia Shang Shiqi Kaogu de Zhuyao Shouhuo (Major Gains of the Xia and Shang Archaeology in Yuxian). *Kaogu yu Wenwu* 1: 40-8.

Zhao, Chunqing (2001) *Zhengluo Diqu Xinshiqi Shidai Juluo de Yanbian*. Beijing Daxue Press, Beijing.

Zhao, Zhiquan (1987) Lun Erlitou Yizhi Wei Xiadai Wanqi Duyi (On the Erlitou Site as a Capital of the Late Xia Dynasty). *Huaxia Kaogu* 2: 196-204, 17.

Zhao, Zhiquan and Diankui Xu (1988) Yanshi Shixianggou Shangdai Zaoqi Chengzhi (Early Shang City at Shixianggou in Yanshi). In *Zhongguo Kaoguxuehui Diwuci Nianhui Lunwenji*, edited by Chinese Archaeology Association. Wenwu Press, Beijing.

Zheng, Guang (1983) Shilun Erlitou Shangdai Zaoqi Wenhua (On the Early Shang Culture at Erlitou). *Zhongguo Kaoguxuehui Disici Nianhui Lunwenji* 4: 18-24.

—— (1996) Erlitou Yizhi de Fajue (Excavations at Erlitou). In *Xia Wenhua Yanjiu Lunji*, edited by Association of Chinese Pre-Qin History, pp. 66-80. Zhonghua Press, Beijing.

—— (1998) Erlitou Yizhi yu Woguo Zaoqi Qingtong Wenming (The Erlitou Site and China's Early Bronze Civilization). In *Zhongguo Kaoguxue Luncong*, edited by Institute of Archaeology, CASS, pp. 190-5. Kexue Press, Beijing.

Zheng, Jiexiang (1994) *Shangdai Dili Gailun*. Zhongzhou Guji Press, Zhengzhou.

Zhengzhou City Cultural Relics Team (1986) Heyi Erfuyuan Dengchu Shangdai Yizhi Fajue Jianbao (Brief Report of Excavations at Heyi Erfuyuan and Other Sites). *Zhongyuan Wenwu* 4: 28-33.

Zhengzhou University, Kaifeng Cultural Relics Team, and Qixian Cultural Relics Management Bureau (1994) Henan Qixian Lutaigang Yizhi Fajue Jianbao (Brief Report of Excavations at the Lutaigang Site in Qixian, Henan). *Kaogu* 8: 673-82.

Zhenjiang City Museum (1978) Jiangsu Jintan Beidun Xi Zhou Mu (Western Zhou Tombs at Beidun in Jintan, Jiangsu). *Kaogu* 3: 151-4.

Zhou, Yan, (2000) Shi 'Xiao Chen' (Interpreting 'Xiao Chen'). *Huaxia Kaogu* 3: 103-6.

Zhou, Yuansheng (1993) Heze Diqu Kaoguxue Wenhua Yicun Shishuo (On Archaeological Remains in the Heze Region). In *Qingguoji*, edited by Archaeology Department of Jilin University, pp. 154-64. Zhishi Press, Beijing.

Zhu, Xun (1999) *Zhongguo Kuangqing: Jinshu Kuangchan*. Kexue Press, Beijing.

Zou, Heng (1979) *Shang Zhou Kaogu*. Wenwu Press, Beijing.

——— (1980) *Xia Shang Zhou Kaogu Lunwenji*. Wenwu Press, Beijing.

——— (1990) Xia Wenhua Yantao de Huigu yu Zhanwang (The Study of the Xia Culture in Retrospect and Prospect). *Zhongyuan Wenwu* 2: 1-12.

——— (1998) Zhengzhou Xiaoshuangqiao Shangdai Yizhi Ao Du Shuo Jibu (Additional Thoughts on the Xiaoshuangqiao Shang Site in Zhengzhou as the Capital City Ao). *Kaogu yu Wenwu* 4: 24-7.

Glossary

Anqiu 安丘

Anyang 安阳

Anyi 安邑

Ba 灞

Baijiazhuang 白家庄

Bainaimiao 白乃庙

Baiyan 白燕

Baiyinchang 白银厂

Baota 宝塔

Beicun 北村

Biedun 鳖墩

Bizigou 蓖子沟

Bohai 渤海

Boqing 亳清

Caoyanzhuang 曹演庄

Chenggu 城固

Chengziya 城子崖

Da yi Shang 大邑商

Daba 大巴

Dabie 大别

Dahangou 大含沟

Dali 大理

Dan 丹

Daxinzhuang 大辛庄

Dayangzhou 大洋州

Daye 大冶

Dayue 大越

Dean 德安

Dexing 德兴

Dinggong 丁公

Dongbei 东北

Dongchuan 东川

Donggou 东沟

Donglongshan 东龙山

Dongmaputou 东马铺头

Dongtan 东滩

Dongting 洞庭

Dongxiafeng 东下冯

Erligang 二里冈

Erlitou 二里头

fang 方

Fantang 繁汤

Fanyang 繁阳

Fen 汾

Fenghuangtai 凤凰台

Fu	福	Houma	侯马
Fucheng	府城	Huai	淮
Funiu	伏牛	Huaize	淮泽
Gan	赣	Huaizhenfang	怀珍坊
Gangou	干沟	Huanbei	洹北
Ganjun	感军	Huayuanzhuang	花园庄
Gaoan	高安	Huixian	辉县
Gaocheng	藁城	Huizui	灰咀
ge	戈	Hujiayu	胡家峪
Gedangtou	圪垱头	Huogeqi	霍各乞
Gongxian	巩县	Ji	济
Gongyi	巩义 (前称巩县)	*jia*	斝
gu	觚	Jiamakou	夹马口
guan	罐	Jiangxian	降县
Guan Zhong	管仲	Jimindu	济民渡
Guang	广	Jin Jiang *ding*	晋姜鼎
Guangfeng	广丰	*jindao xihang*	金道锡行
guo	国	Jingzhou	荆州
Gutangdun	古塘墩	Jinnanshi	荆南寺
Han	汉	Jinshui	金水
Hankou	含口	*Jiu Tang shu*	旧唐书
Hedong	河东	Jiujiang	九江
Heihe	黑河	Jiuzhou	九州
Heze	荷泽	*jiwokuang*	鸡窝矿
Hongyan	红岩	Jiyuan	济源

jue	爵	Mang	邙
kuixingqi	盔形器	Mangling	邙岭
Lantian	蓝田	Mangzhang	蟒张
Laoniupo	老牛坡	Maojindu	茅津渡
Leping	乐平	Mayang	麻阳
li	鬲	*meijin*	美金
Li	澧	Mengzhuang	孟庄
Liao	辽	Mianyangdi	眠羊地
Lihe	李河	Minggonglu	铭功路
Lijiazui	李家咀	Muyushan	木鱼山
Lijin	利津	Nanguan	南关
Linru	临汝	Nanguanwai	南关外
Longshan	龙山	Nanhegou	南河沟
Longwangling	龙王岭	Nanyang	南阳
Louziwan	楼子湾	Panlong	盘龙
lu	卤	Panlongcheng	盘龙城
lu xiao chen	卤小臣	Pinglu	平陆
lu xiao chen qi you yi		Pingxiang	萍乡
卤小臣其有邑		Poyang	鄱阳
Luo	洛	Qi	淇
Luojiahe	落家河	Qi	齐
Lushan	鲁山	Qianshan	铅山
Lushi	卢氏	Qin	沁
Lutaigang	鹿台岗	Qing	清
Luyang	鲁阳	Qinglong	青龙

Qingzhou	青州	Taigu	太谷
Qinling	秦岭	Taihang	太行
Qixian	杞县	Taixi	台西
Quli	曲里	Tang	唐
Renmingongyuan	人民公园	Tanyaokou	炭窑口
Rongsheng	戎生	Tongbai	桐柏
Ru	汝	Tonggushan	铜鼓山
Ruichang	瑞昌	Tongjiazui	童家咀
Sanxingdui	三星堆	Tongkuangyu	铜矿峪
Sha	沙	Tongling (Anhui)	铜陵
Shangshu	尚书	Tongling (Jiangxi)	铜岭
Shangzhou	商州	Tonglushan	铜绿山
Shaochai	稍柴	Tu	土
Shihuishan	石灰山	Tubo	土蕃
Shiji	史记	Wangjiazui	王家咀
Shimen	石门	Wannian	万年
Shu	蜀	Wei	渭
Shuijingzhu	水经注	Weigang	桅岗
Si	泗	*weng*	瓮
situ	四土	Wenxi	闻喜
Siziwangqi	四子王旗	Wucheng	吴城
Song	嵩	Wulatehouqi	乌拉特后旗
Song Shi	宋史	Wuluo	坞罗
Su	涑	Wuyi	武夷
Tai	太	Wuzhi	武陟

179

Xiao	崤	Yanshi	偃师
Xiao	萧	Yaoxian	耀县
xiao chen	小臣	*ye*	野
Xiaoqing	小清	Yi	伊
Xiaoshuangqiao	小双桥	*yi*	邑
Xiaotun	小屯	Yicheng	翼城
Xiaoxigou	小西沟	Yi-Luo	伊洛
Xiaqiyuan	下七垣	Yimen	易门
Xia-Shang-Zhou	夏商周	Yin	阴
Xiawanggang	下王岗	Ying	颍
Xichuan	淅川	Yinxu	殷墟
Xie	解	Yongji	永济
Xincai	新蔡	*you yi*	有邑
Xing Tang Shu	新唐书	Yuan	沅
Xin'gan	新干	Yuanqu	垣曲
Xinyu	新余	*Yuanquxian dianxiayang* 垣曲县店下样	
Xinzhai	新砦		
Xionger	熊耳	Yueshi	岳石
Xixia	西夏	*Yugong*	禹贡
Xuzhou	徐州	Yuncheng	运城
Ya	鸭	Yuxian	蔚县
yan	甗	Zaoshi	皂市
Yangjiawan	杨家湾	*Zengbo Qi fu*	曾伯秉簠
Yangjiuzui	杨家咀	Zhanghe	漳河
Yangzhuang	杨庄	Zhangshu	樟树
		Zhangshutan	樟树潭

180

Zhaopu	赵舖	Zhukaigou	朱开沟
Zhengzhou Yanchang 郑州烟厂		Zijingshan	紫荆山
		Zouping	邹平
Zhongtiao	中条	*zun*	尊
Zhugan	竹竿		

Index

183

Index

Index